PRAISE FOR THE
FIRST EDITION

These truly are twenty basic beliefs that every Christian should know. Wayne Grudem is a master teacher with the ability to explain profound truths in simple language. He is a man of deep conviction and theological passion—and those who read this book will be both educated and encouraged in the faith.

R. Albert Mohler Jr., Southern Baptist
Theological Seminary, Louisville, Kentucky

Based on *Systematic Theology*, this summary will certainly help beginners with Christ to get the hang of their faith.

J. I. Packer†, Regent College,
Vancouver, British Columbia

As Wayne Grudem's *Systematic Theology* contracts into a compact book, I do not lose my enthusiasm for the truth he loves and the clarity of his words.

John Piper, Bethlehem Baptist Church,
Minneapolis, Minnesota

Christian Beliefs

Christian Beliefs

Twenty Basics Every Christian Should Know

Second Edition

Wayne Grudem
Edited by Elliot Grudem

INTER-VARSITY PRESS
36 Causton Street, London SW1P 4ST, England
Email: ivp@ivpbooks.com
Website: www.ivpbooks.com

This book is published jointly with Zondervan Academic, 3900 Sparks Dr. SE, Grand Rapids, Michigan 49546, USA.

First published 2005
Second edition published 2022

British Library Cataloguing-in-Publication Data
A catalogue record for this book is available from the British Library.

ISBN: 978–1–78974–419–4

Typeset in the United States of America
Printed and bound in Great Britain by Ashford Colour Press Ltd, Gosport, Hampshire

Produced on paper from sustainable sources

Inter-Varsity Press publishes Christian books that are true to the Bible and that communicate the gospel, develop discipleship and strengthen the church for its mission in the world.

IVP originated within the Inter-Varsity Fellowship, now the Universities and Colleges Christian Fellowship, a student movement connecting Christian Unions in universities and colleges throughout Great Britain, and a member movement of the International Fellowship of Evangelical Students. Website: www.uccf.org.uk. That historic association is maintained, and all senior IVP staff and committee members subscribe to the UCCF Basis of Faith.

With thanks to God for the life and memory
of Rachael R. Freeman Grudem

Born June 2, 1982
Married to Alexander Grudem April 3, 2005
Died July 9, 2005

And Job said, "The LORD gave, and the LORD has taken away; blessed be the name of the LORD."
            —*Job 1:21*

And we know that for those who love God all things work together for good, for those who are called according to his purpose.
            —*Romans 8:28*

"He will wipe away every tear from their eyes, and death shall be no more, neither shall there be mourning nor crying, nor pain anymore, for the former things have passed away."
            —*Revelation 21:4*

CONTENTS

PREFACE TO THE SECOND EDITION

I am grateful to God for the way he has been pleased to use the first edition of this book to introduce thousands of people to the basic doctrines of the Christian faith.

This second edition was necessary in order to reflect some of the changes in my book *Systematic Theology*, second edition, which was published in December 2020 (1,586 pages). However, while the modifications and additions to *Systematic Theology* were substantial, most of the changes dealt with finer points of doctrine, and very few of them affected my handling of the twenty basic Christian beliefs found in this book. Therefore, the changes to this book are few, and they primarily involve a stronger treatment of the inerrancy of Scripture, a brief description of liberal Protestantism and its view of Scripture, a more extensive treatment of the clarity of Scripture, a significantly revised bibliography, and a number of small corrections elsewhere in the book.

Once again I am grateful for the editorial work of my son Elliot Grudem, founding president of Leaders Collective (a ministry focused on pastoral longevity), and assistant pastor at Christ the King Presbyterian Church (PCA) in Raleigh, North Carolina, who did an excellent job of composing the changes to this book. However, I am responsible for the final wording of the manuscript. I am also grateful to Brett Gray for his help in proofreading, to Jonathan Poland for preparing the indexes, and to Matt Estel of Zondervan for outstanding editorial help.

This book, like the first edition, is dedicated to the memory of Rachael Grudem, first wife of Alexander Grudem (my son and Elliot's brother), who died in a tragic car accident as we were finishing the first edition. Since that time, Alexander has married Lauren (Demianiuk), whom we have joyfully welcomed into our family. And on March 5, 2020, Alexander and Lauren welcomed into the world Margaret Irene Grudem, our fourth grandchild. Our faith in the doctrines discussed in this book continues to deepen, both in times of sorrow and in times of joy, as does our faith in God, "who works all things according to the counsel of his will" (Eph. 1:11).

Wayne Grudem, Scottsdale, Arizona
February 15, 2021

PREFACE TO THE FIRST EDITION

This book is a summary of twenty basic beliefs that every Christian should know.

It is a condensed version of my book *Bible Doctrine* (528 pages), and that itself is a condensed version of my *Systematic Theology* (1,290 pages).[1] My son Elliot Grudem, an MDiv graduate from Reformed Theological Seminary in Orlando, Florida, has done an excellent job in saving the most essential sections from those earlier books, condensing long discussions into a key sentence or two, and revising some of the wording to make it understandable even for people who are brand-new to the Christian faith. I then edited the manuscript lightly, and the responsibility for the final wording is mine alone. (I am also grateful for the work of Steve Eriksson and Robert Polen, who helped with proofreading, and Chris Davis, who prepared the index.)

I hope this shorter book will be useful for new Christians, for new members' classes in churches, for home and college

---

1. Wayne Grudem, *Bible Doctrine: Essential Teachings of the Christian Faith*, ed. Jeff Purswell (Grand Rapids: Zondervan; Leicester, UK: Inter-Varsity Press, 1999); and Wayne Grudem, *Systematic Theology: An Introduction to Biblical Doctrine* (Grand Rapids: Zondervan; Leicester, UK: Inter-Varsity Press, 1994).

Bible study groups, and even for Sunday school classes for children from about age thirteen on up. It should also be helpful for non-Christians looking for a brief summary of basic Christian teachings.

The two comments I hear most frequently from people who have read *Systematic Theology* or *Bible Doctrine* are "Thank you for writing a theology book that I can understand" and "This book is helping my Christian life." We have attempted to preserve those two qualities—clarity and application to life—in this condensed book as well.

We have kept a strong focus on the Bible as the source for what Christians believe. Instead of just citing references to Bible verses, we have frequently quoted actual verses from the Bible, because God's very words are "living and active, sharper than any two-edged sword, piercing to the division of soul and of spirit, of joints and of marrow, and discerning the thoughts and intentions of the heart" (Heb. 4:12). The words of the Bible nourish us spiritually. Paul says that the Word of God is "able to build you up" (Acts 20:32), and Jesus says, "Man shall not live by bread alone, but by every word that comes from the mouth of God" (Matt. 4:4).[2]

Knowing and understanding basic Christian beliefs is important for every Christian. People who don't know what the Bible teaches will have no ability to distinguish truth from error, and they will be like "children, tossed to and fro by the waves and carried about by every wind of doctrine" (Eph. 4:14). But Christians who have a solid foundation will be maturer, will not be easily led astray, will have better judgment, and will

---

2. All Bible quotations are taken from the *English Standard Version* unless otherwise noted. Italics in Scripture quotes have been added by the author.

"have their powers of discernment trained by constant practice to distinguish good from evil" (Heb. 5:14).

We have dedicated this book to the memory of Rachael Grudem, who died instantly in a tragic car accident in St. Paul, Minnesota, on July 9, 2005. Rachael constantly radiated joy and faith in her Lord Jesus Christ and love for her husband of three months, Alexander Grudem, who is Wayne's son and Elliot's brother. In the midst of our family's sadness, God has deepened our faith in the doctrines we discuss in this book, especially our assurance that God is good and wise, that Rachael is in heaven rejoicing, and that we will someday be with her in God's presence forever.

Wayne Grudem, Scottsdale, Arizona
Elliot Grudem, Raleigh, North Carolina
July 27, 2005

ABBREVIATIONS
OF BIBLE BOOKS

Old Testament		New Testament	
Gen.	Genesis	Matt.	Matthew
Ex.	Exodus	Mark	Mark
Lev.	Leviticus	Luke	Luke
Num.	Numbers	John	John
Deut.	Deuteronomy	Acts	Acts
Josh.	Joshua	Rom.	Romans
Judg.	Judges	1 Cor.	1 Corinthians
Ruth	Ruth	2 Cor.	2 Corinthians
1 Sam.	1 Samuel	Gal.	Galatians
2 Sam.	2 Samuel	Eph.	Ephesians
1 Kings	1 Kings	Phil.	Philippians
2 Kings	2 Kings	Col.	Colossians
1 Chron.	1 Chronicles	1 Thess.	1 Thessalonians
2 Chron.	2 Chronicles	2 Thess.	2 Thessalonians
Ezra	Ezra	1 Tim.	1 Timothy
Neh.	Nehemiah	2 Tim.	2 Timothy
Est.	Esther	Titus	Titus
Job	Job	Philem.	Philemon
Ps. (Pss.)	Psalm(s)	Heb.	Hebrews

Old Testament		New Testament	
Prov.	Proverbs	James	James
Eccl.	Ecclesiastes	1 Peter	1 Peter
Song	Song of Songs	2 Peter	2 Peter
Isa.	Isaiah	1 John	1 John
Jer.	Jeremiah	2 John	2 John
Lam.	Lamentations	3 John	3 John
Ezek.	Ezekiel	Jude	Jude
Dan.	Daniel	Rev.	Revelation
Hos.	Hosea		
Joel	Joel		
Amos	Amos		
Obad.	Obadiah		
Jonah	Jonah		
Mic.	Micah		
Nah.	Nahum		
Hab.	Habakkuk		
Zeph.	Zephaniah		
Hag.	Haggai		
Zech.	Zechariah		
Mal.	Malachi		

chapter 1

WHAT IS THE BIBLE?

Any responsible look at a single Christian belief should be based on what God says about that subject. Therefore, as we begin to look at a series of basic Christian beliefs, it makes sense to start with the basis for these beliefs—God's words, or the Bible. One topic the Bible thoroughly covers is itself; that is, the Bible tells us what God thinks about his very words. God's opinion of his words can be broken down into four general categories: authority, clarity, necessity, and sufficiency.

The Authority of the Bible

All the words in the Bible are God's words. Therefore, to disbelieve or disobey them is to disbelieve or disobey God himself. Oftentimes passages in the Old Testament are introduced with the phrase, "Thus says the LORD" (see Ex. 4:22; Josh. 24:2; 1 Sam. 10:18; Isa. 10:24; also Deut. 18:18–20; Jer. 1:9). This phrase, understood to be like the command of a king, indicated that what followed was to be obeyed without challenge or question. Even the words in the Old Testament not attributed as direct quotes from God are considered to be God's words. Paul, in 2 Timothy 3:16, makes this clear when he writes that "all Scripture is breathed out by God."

1

The New Testament also affirms that its words are the very words of God. In 2 Peter 3:16 Peter refers to all of Paul's letters as one part of the "Scriptures." This means that Peter, and the early church, considered Paul's writings to be in the same category as the Old Testament writings. Therefore, they considered Paul's writings to be the very words of God.

In addition, Paul, in 1 Timothy 5:18, writes that "the Scripture says" two things: "You shall not muzzle an ox when it treads out the grain," and "The laborer deserves his wages." The first quote, regarding an ox, comes from the Old Testament; it is found in Deuteronomy 25:4. The second comes from the New Testament; it is found in Luke 10:7. Paul, without any hesitation, quotes from both the Old and New Testaments, calling them both "Scripture." Therefore, again, the words of the New Testament are considered to be the very words of God. That is why Paul could write, "The things I am writing to you are a command of the Lord" (1 Cor. 14:37).

Since the Old and New Testament writings are both considered Scripture, it is right to say they are both, in the words of 2 Timothy 3:16, "breathed out by God." This makes sense when we consider Jesus' promise that the Holy Spirit would "bring to" the disciples' "remembrance" all that Jesus said to them (John 14:26). It was as the disciples wrote the Spirit-enabled words that books such as Matthew, John, and 1 and 2 Peter were written.

The Bible says there are "many ways" (Heb. 1:1) in which the actual words of the Bible were written. Sometimes God spoke directly to the author, who simply recorded what he heard (Rev. 2:1, 8, 12). At other times, the author based much of his writings on interviews and research (Luke 1:1–3). And at yet other times, the Holy Spirit brought to mind things that Jesus taught (John 14:26). Regardless of the way the words came to the authors, the words they put down were an extension of them—their personalities, skills, backgrounds, and training. But they were also exactly the words God wanted them to write.

Though every word in the Bible was written by a human person, the words are more than merely human writings. They are also the very words of God himself, the very words God claims as his own.

This view—that the human words of the Bible are also God's very words to us—is the primary difference between Bible-believing (or evangelical) Protestant theology and liberal Protestant theology. People who hold to liberal Protestant theology would say that the words of the Bible are merely human words that bear witness to some ancient writers' understandings of their experience of God, and therefore they might be inconsistent or contradictory or untrustworthy in various places.

If God claims that the words of Scripture are his own, then there is ultimately no higher authority one can appeal to for proof of this claim than Scripture itself. For what authority could be higher than God? So, Scripture ultimately gains its authority from itself. But the claims of Scripture only become our personal convictions through the work of the Holy Spirit in our individual hearts.

The Holy Spirit doesn't change the words of Scripture in any way; he doesn't supernaturally make them become the words of God (for they always have been). He does, however, change the reader of Scripture. The Holy Spirit makes readers realize the Bible is unlike any book they have ever read. Through reading, they believe that the words of Scripture are the very words of God himself. It is as Jesus said in John 10:27: "My sheep hear my voice . . . and they follow me." Other kinds of arguments (such as historical reliability, internal consistency, fulfilled prophecies, influence on others, and the majestic beauty and wisdom of the content) can be useful in helping us see the reasonableness of the claims of the Bible.

As God's very words, the words of Scripture are more than simply true; they are truth itself (John 17:17). They are the final measure by which all supposed truth is to be gauged. Therefore, that which conforms to Scripture is true; that which doesn't conform to Scripture is not true. New scientific or historical facts may cause us to reexamine our interpretation of Scripture, but they will never directly contradict Scripture.

The truth of the Scriptures does not demand that the Bible report events with exact scientific detail (though all the details it does report are true). For example, in Matthew 13:32 Jesus says that a mustard seed "is the smallest of all seeds." Jesus was not speaking to a group of modern seed scientists but to a group of first-century agrarian people. They would understand *seed* to refer to an agricultural seed planted in the ground to grow crops. In that sense, Jesus spoke truly and rightly.

The truth of the Scriptures also doesn't demand that the Bible tell us everything we need to know or ever could know about a subject. It never makes either of these claims. For example, Acts 5:34–39 records a speech by a Pharisee named Gamaliel, in which he talks about two Jewish revolutionaries, Theudas and Judas. Luke records Gamaliel claiming the Theudas-led revolution came before the Judas-led revolution. This seems to contradict the account of the Jewish historian Josephus, who wrote in AD 95 that a Judas-led revolution came before a Theudas-led revolution.

This apparent contradiction doesn't require us to admit

an error in the Scriptures, however. It could be that Josephus, writing fifty years later, made a mistake about the order. Or it could be that Gamaliel and Josephus are writing about two different revolutionaries named Theudas (which was not a rare name then).

The Bible was written by ordinary men in an ordinary language with an ordinary style. Therefore, it does contain loose or free quotations and some uncommon and unusual forms of grammar or spelling. However, these are not matters of truthfulness. The Bible does not, in its original form, affirm anything contrary to fact.

If the Bible does affirm something contrary to fact, then it cannot be trusted. And if the Bible cannot be trusted, then God himself cannot be trusted. To believe that the Bible affirms something false would be to disbelieve God himself. To disbelieve God himself is to place yourself as a higher authority with a deeper, more developed understanding on a topic or topics than God himself.

Therefore, since the Bible affirms that it is the very words of God, we are to seek to understand those words, for in doing so, we are seeking to understand God himself. We are to seek to trust the words of Scripture, for in doing so, we are seeking to trust God himself. And we are to seek to obey the words of Scripture, for in doing so, we are seeking to obey God himself.

The Clarity of Scripture

As we read Scripture and seek to understand and obey it, we discover that some passages are easier to understand than others. Peter affirmed this when he wrote the following about Paul's letters: "There are some things in them that are hard to understand" (2 Peter 3:16).

That said, you don't need an advanced degree to understand the teachings of Scripture. For over and over again the Scriptures affirm that the Bible is written in a way that is understandable for all Christians. Right understanding requires time, effort, the help of the Holy Spirit, and obedience. Though we won't understand everything rightly in our lifetime, we can understand a remarkably large amount of the Bible's teachings.

Although there are some mysteries in Scripture, they should not overwhelm us. For "the testimony of the LORD is sure, making wise the simple" (Ps. 19:7). And "the unfolding" of God's "words gives light; it imparts understanding to the simple" (Ps. 119:130). God's Word is so understandable and clear that even the simple (people who lack sound judgment) can be made wise by it.

In Deuteronomy 6:1–9 we read that God commanded Moses to teach God's law to God's people. They were expected to understand, internalize, and obey it. This allowed each Israelite to teach God's words "diligently" to their children (Deut. 6:7) so their children could understand, internalize, and obey them. The expectation was that this pattern would continue through each generation. Moses taught God's people, and then he died. God's people continued to listen to the public reading of God's words (what we now call the Old Testament) and continued to teach what they understood to their children.

Jesus assumes a right understanding of God's Word in answering the challenges of the Pharisees (religious scholars), for he often starts with a phrase like "Have you not read in the Law . . ." (Matt. 12:5). The letters that make up the majority of the New Testament were most often written and read to the entire church (not just scholars and leaders), which would include both adults and children.

Both Jesus and the New Testament writers expect their original audience not only to know what the Old Testament taught but also to understand and obey it, even though they were living over a thousand years after much of it was originally written. Christians today, now two thousand years removed from the original audience of the New Testament, are expected to be able to understand all the Scriptures as well.

Though Peter affirmed some of Paul's teachings were "hard to understand" (2 Peter 3:16), he didn't say they could never be understood. Christians need to put in time and effort to rightly understand the Bible. We are to "delight" in it and meditate on it "day and night" (Ps. 1:2). Understanding of Scripture doesn't come at once but can increase over a lifetime. It doesn't just take time; it also takes effort. The Bible presents Ezra as a model priest who put in effort to understand God's Word: he "set his heart to study the Law of the LORD" (Ezra 7:10) so he could obey it and teach it. If Christians want to understand the Bible well, they need to put in the time and effort to do so, by reading it in a translation they can understand, listening to their pastor preach biblical sermons, reading books and commentaries about the Bible, studying what the church believed about biblical teaching throughout history, and talking with fellow believers about it.

We do not arrive at an understanding of God's Word on our own. We need God to open our minds "to understand the Scriptures" (Luke 24:45), for the things of God are "spiritually discerned" (1 Cor. 2:14). Like Jesus' disciples, we need the help of the Holy Spirit to "teach" us "all things" (John 14:26). The Holy Spirit is given to us "that we might understand the things freely given us by God" (1 Cor. 2:12).

A right understanding of Scripture is often more the

result of our spiritual condition than our intellectual ability. Disobeying God can hinder our fellowship with the Holy Spirit (Eph. 4:30). Obeying God deepens our fellowship with the Holy Spirit and our understanding of God and his Word. This is why the truth of Scripture often appears to be "folly" to those who reject the claims of Jesus (1 Cor. 2:14). In contrast, those who love God pray prayers like the ones found in the Psalms: "Open my eyes, that I may behold wondrous things out of your law" (Ps. 119:18), and "Give me understanding, that I may keep your law and observe it with my whole heart" (Ps. 119:34). The Holy Spirit helps us understand and obey the Bible. Our obedience increases our fellowship with the Holy Spirit and our understanding of the Bible.

This does not mean, however, that every Bible-related misunderstanding is due to a person's spiritual condition. There are many people—many godly, Christian people—who have greatly misunderstood some part of Scripture. Often the disciples misunderstood what Jesus was talking about (see Matt. 15:16, for example). Sometimes this was due to their hardened hearts (Luke 24:25); at other times it was because they needed to wait for further events and understanding (John 12:16). In addition, members of the early church did not always agree on the meaning of what was written in Scripture (see Acts 15 and Gal. 2:11–14 for examples of this).

When individuals disagree on the proper interpretation of a passage of Scripture, the problem does not lie with Scripture, for God guided its composition so that it could be understood. Rather, the problem lies with us. Sometimes, as a result of our shortcomings, we fail to properly understand what the Bible is teaching. Even so, we should prayerfully read the Bible, asking the Lord to reveal the truth of his words to us.

The Necessity of Scripture

We need God to reveal the truth of his words to us so we can know what it means to become a Christian, live as a Christian, and grow as a Christian. Without the Bible we could not know these things. The necessity of Scripture means that it is necessary to read the Bible or have someone tell us what is in the Bible if we are going to know God personally, have our sins forgiven, and know with certainty what God wants us to do.

Paul hints at this when he asks how anyone can hear about becoming a Christian "without someone preaching" (Rom. 10:14). For "faith comes from hearing, and hearing through the word of Christ" (Rom. 10:17). If no one is preaching the word of Christ, Paul says, people won't be saved. And that word comes from the Scriptures. So in order to know how to become a Christian, ordinarily one must either read about it in the Bible or have someone else explain what the Bible says about it. As Paul told Timothy, "The sacred writings . . . are able to make you wise for salvation through faith in Christ Jesus" (2 Tim. 3:15).

The Christian life not only starts with the Bible but also thrives through the Bible. Jesus said in Matthew 4:4, "Man shall not live by bread alone, but by every word that comes from the mouth of God." Just as our physical lives are maintained by daily nourishment with physical food, so our spiritual lives are maintained by daily nourishment with the Word of God. To neglect regular reading of the Bible is detrimental to the health of our souls.

In addition, the Bible is our only source for clear and definite statements about God's will. While God has not revealed all aspects of his will to us—for "the secret things belong to the LORD our God"—many aspects of his will are revealed to us through the Scriptures, "that we may do all the words of this law" (Deut. 29:29). Love for God is demonstrated by keeping "his commandments" (1 John 5:3). And his commandments are found on the pages of Scripture.

While the Bible is necessary for many things, it is not needed for knowing some things about God, such as his character and his moral laws, for "the heavens declare the glory of God, and the sky above proclaims his handiwork" (Ps. 19:1). Paul says that even for the wicked, "what can be known about God is plain to them, because God has shown it to them" (Rom. 1:19). Not only do the wicked know of God and about God, but they also have in their minds and consciences some understanding of God's moral laws (Rom. 1:32; 2:14–15).

Therefore, this "general revelation" about God's existence, character, and moral law is given to all people; it is seen through nature, God's historical works, and an inner sense that God has placed in everyone. It is called "general revelation" because it is given to all people in general. It is distinct from the Bible. By contrast, "special revelation" is God's revelation to specific people. The entire Bible is special revelation, and so are the direct messages from God to the prophets and others as recorded in the Bible's historical stories.

The Sufficiency of Scripture

Although those alive during the Old Testament period didn't have the benefit of God's complete revelation, which is found in the New Testament, they had access to all the words of God that he intended them to have during their lives. Today the Bible contains all the words of God a person needs to become a Christian, live as a Christian, and grow as a Christian. In order to be "blameless" before God, we just have to obey his

Word: "Blessed are those whose way is *blameless*, who walk in the law of the LORD!" (Ps. 119:1). And in the Bible God has given us instructions that equip us for "every good work" he wants us to do (2 Tim. 3:16–17). This is what it means to say that Scripture is "sufficient."

Consequently, it is in Scripture alone that we search for God's words to us. And we should, eventually, arrive at contentment with what we find there. The sufficiency of Scripture should encourage us to search through the Bible to try to find what God would have us think about a certain issue or do in a certain situation. Everything God wants to tell all his people for all time about that kind of issue or situation will be found on the pages of the Bible. While the Bible might not directly answer every question we can think up—for "the secret things belong to the LORD our God" (Deut. 29:29)—it will provide us with the guidance we need "for every good work" (2 Tim. 3:17).

When we don't find the specific answer to a specific question in the Bible, we are not free to add to the commands of Scripture what we have found to be pragmatically correct. It is certainly possible that God will give us specific guidance in particular day-to-day situations, but we do not have license to place on par with Scripture any modern revelations, leadings, or other forms of guidance that we believe to be from God. Nor should we ever seek to impose such guidance on other Christians generally or on other people in our churches, since we can be wrong about such guidance and God never wants us to give it the status of his words in the Bible.

There are some issues and situations for which God has not provided the precise direction or rules that we may desire. But because Scripture is sufficient, we do not have the right to add to its commands or teachings. For example, while it may be appropriate for one church to meet at a certain time on Sunday morning, it could be completely appropriate for another church to meet at a different time, because the Bible does not speak directly to the issue of Sunday service times. If one church told the other that they needed to meet at a certain hour, that church would be in sin and would not be demonstrating a belief in the sufficiency of Scripture.

In the same way, with regard to living the Christian life, the sufficiency of Scripture reminds us that nothing is sin that is not forbidden by Scripture either explicitly or by implication. Therefore, we are not to add prohibitions where we don't believe Scripture is precise enough. From time to time, for example, there may be situations where it is inappropriate for a Christian to drink caffeine, attend a movie theater, or eat meat offered to idols (see 1 Cor. 8–10). But since there isn't any specific teaching or some general principle of Scripture that forbids these actions by all Christians at all times, these activities are not in themselves sinful.

Therefore, in our doctrinal, ethical, and moral teachings and beliefs, we should be content with what God has told us in Scripture. God has revealed exactly what he knows is right for us. Many differences that have divided churches and denominations are issues on which the Bible places little emphasis. Many individual conclusions on issues like the proper form of church government, the exact nature of Christ's presence in the Lord's Supper, or the exact nature and order of the events surrounding Christ's return are drawn more from skillful inference than from direct biblical statements. One should, therefore, exhibit a humble hesitancy in placing more emphasis on these issues than the Bible does.

Questions for Review and Application

1. Why is it important that the Bible be the basis for our beliefs?
2. Will the Bible definitively answer every question we bring to it? Why or why not?
3. What is one issue that the Bible speaks clearly on? What is one issue that the Bible does not speak clearly on? How does this affect the emphasis you should place on these issues?

chapter 2

WHAT IS GOD LIKE?

Just as Scripture is the highest source of information about itself, God is the highest source of information about himself. That makes sense, for if there was a higher source of information about God, then God wouldn't be God. Therefore, it is important that any study of God look at what God says about himself—in the pages of Scripture.

God Exists

Scripture simply assumes God exists. The first verse of the Bible—"In the beginning, *God* created the heavens and the earth" (Gen. 1:1)—matter-of-factly presents God as Creator without any proof for his existence or actions.

Scripture also tells us that all persons everywhere have a deep, inner sense that God exists, that they are his creatures and that he is their Creator. In Romans 1:19 Paul writes that even for the wicked, this sense is "plain to them, because God has shown it to them." Although many today do not acknowledge that God exists, Paul says this is because "they exchanged the truth about God for a lie" (Rom. 1:25), therefore actively or willingly rejecting some truth about God's character and existence that they originally knew. In essence, they convince themselves that "there is no God" (Ps. 10:4).

The knowledge of God that Paul refers to can be "clearly perceived . . . in the things that have been made" (Rom. 1:20). Every created thing gives evidence of God and his character. But human beings—created in the image of God—give the most evidence of God's existence and character.

Therefore, belief in God is not some "blind faith"; it is based on evidence found both in the Bible and in the natural world.

God Is Knowable

Not only does God exist, but he exists in such a way that we can know things about him and come to know him personally.

We will, however, never fully know God. He is infinite and we are finite. "His greatness is unsearchable," too great ever to be fully known (Ps. 145:3). "His understanding is beyond measure" (Ps. 147:5). God's knowledge is "too wonderful" for us; it is so high we "cannot attain it" (Ps. 139:6), and if we could count God's thoughts, we would find them greater in number than the sands of the earth (Ps. 139:17–18). While we will never fully know God, we can *personally* know God. Jesus said eternal life was found in knowing him and knowing "the only true God" who sent him (John 17:3). This is far better than simply knowing about God. In fact, in Jeremiah 9:24 God says, "Let him who boasts boast in this, that he understands and *knows me*."

In addition to knowing God, we can know about him from what he tells us about himself on the pages of Scripture. For example, Scripture tells us that God is love (1 John 4:8), God is light (1 John 1:5), God is spirit (John 4:24), and God is righteous (Rom. 3:26). Some of God's attributes are easier to understand because they are attributes he shares with us; others are more difficult to grasp because they are attributes that he doesn't share with us. Because we are finite creations of an infinite Creator, we will never fully understand everything there is to understand about any one of God's attributes. Even so, there is tremendous value in learning God's attributes, for in them we will find the true things about God that he wants us to know. And as people created for God's glory (Isa. 43:7), we can bring him glory as we imitate him by exhibiting likeness to his attributes.

God Is Independent

God's independence means he doesn't actually *need* us or anything else in creation for anything. He did not create us because he was lonely or needed fellowship with people. God always has been perfectly and completely happy and fulfilled in his personal existence. Paul says in Acts 17:24–25, "The God who made the world and everything in it . . . does not live in temples made by man, nor is he served by human hands, *as though he needed anything*, since he himself gives to all mankind life and breath and everything."

God always was. He was not created; he never came into being. The psalmist writes, "Before the mountains were brought forth, or ever you had formed the earth and the world, from everlasting to everlasting you are God" (Ps. 90:2). Therefore, God is not dependent on anyone for anything. Indeed, because he is God, he *cannot* be dependent on anyone or anything. Instead, his entire creation is and must be dependent on him. "For from him and through him and to him are all things" (Rom. 11:36).

Though God is completely independent, he *chooses* to give us value and significance. He allows us to be important to him! Indeed, all creation glorifies and brings him joy. As he says in Isaiah 43:7, "Everyone who is called by my name . . . I created for my glory." And Zephaniah says God "will rejoice" over us "with gladness" and "exult" over us "with loud singing" (Zeph. 3:17). Although God does not need us, he allows us to bring joy to his heart—joy that results in loud singing! That is a sign of true significance.

God Is Unchangeable

God is unchangeable, but not in every way we might think him to be. Instead, he is unchangeable only in the ways the Scriptures tell us he is unchangeable: God is unchangeable in his *being, attributes, purposes, and promises.* The psalmist praises God for being the same (Ps. 102:27). God affirms this when he, in reference to his attributes, says that he does not change: "For I the LORD do not change" (Mal. 3:6). When God stays the same in his being and attributes, it is in direct contrast to us: Our beings will change and our attributes will change. God, on the other hand, will stay the same forever.

In addition, God is unchangeable in his purposes. Once he has determined he will bring something about, it will be achieved. For "the counsel of the LORD stands forever, the plans of his heart to all generations" (Ps. 33:11). His individual plans for eternity (such as those found in Matthew 25:34 and Ephesians 1:4, 11) will come to pass.

God is also unchanging in his promises. As is written in Numbers 23:19, "God is not man, that he should lie, or a son of man, that he should change his mind. Has he said, and will he not do it? Or has he spoken, and will he not fulfill it?"

Even so, there are places in Scripture that seem at first to contradict God's unchangeableness—especially related to his purposes and promises. For example, when the people of Nineveh repented, God did not punish them as promised (Jonah 3:4, 10; for other examples, see Ex. 32:9–14 and Isa. 38:1–6). But these instances should be understood as true expressions of God's *present* attitude or intention related to *the specific situation.* As the situation changes, God's attitude or expression of an intention will change as well.

God's unchangeableness does not mean he will not act nor feel differently in response to different situations (for he would hardly be good or just if he did not respond differently to sin than to repentance and righteousness). Nor does unchangeableness mean God doesn't act or feel emotions. In fact, one of the ways God demonstrates that he is "God and not a man" is by not executing his "burning anger" and destroying a people; instead, as his "heart recoils within" him and his "compassion grows warm and tender," God withholds his judgment and says "I will not come in wrath" (Hos. 11:8–9).

God Is Eternal

God, being eternal, has no beginning or end or succession of events in his own being. This is affirmed in Psalm 90:2: "Before the mountains were brought forth, or ever you had formed the earth and the world, from everlasting to everlasting you are God." He was working "before the foundation of the world" (Eph. 1:4). He has always existed. He is the first and last, the beginning and the end, "the Alpha and the Omega . . . who is and who was and who is to come" (Rev. 1:8). Jude tells us that "glory, majesty, dominion, and authority" were God's "before all time" as well as "now and forever" (Jude 25).

Because God is eternal, his view of time is radically different from ours. For example, "a thousand years" are in his sight "but as yesterday when it is past, or as a watch in the night" (Ps. 90:4). Therefore, all of past history is to God as if it just happened. Peter affirms this when he writes "With the Lord . . . a thousand years" is "as one day" (2 Peter 3:8). But Peter also tells us one day seems to last forever to God: "With the Lord one day is as a thousand years" (2 Peter 3:8).

Taken together, these perspectives let us know that God views the whole span of history as vividly as he would if it were a brief event that had just happened. But he also views a brief event as if it were going on forever. God sees and knows all events—past, present, and future—with equal vividness. Although he has no succession of movements, he still sees the progression of events at different points in time. And as the One who created and rules over time, God uses time for his own purposes.

God Is Omnipresent

Just as God is unlimited with regard to time, he is also unlimited with regard to space. He is omnipresent. He does not have size or spatial dimensions; he is present in every point of space with his whole being. He cannot be limited by material space because he created it (Gen. 1:1).

God is also present in every part of space; he is everywhere; he fills heaven and earth (Jer. 23:23–24). As David writes, "Where shall I go from your Spirit? Or where shall I flee from your presence? If I ascend to heaven, you are there! If I make my bed in Sheol, you are there! If I take the wings of the morning and dwell in the uttermost parts of the sea, even there your hand shall lead me, and your right hand shall hold me" (Ps. 139:7–10). God is present in every part of space, but his being is such that even "heaven and the highest heaven cannot contain" him (1 Kings 8:27).

Although God is present everywhere, he is present and acts in different ways in different places. Often God is present to bless, as is described in Psalm 16:11: "In your presence there is fullness of joy; at your right hand are pleasures forevermore." At other times and places, like hell, for example, God is present not to show any blessing but only to punish and thereby manifest his justice (Amos 9:1–4).

And sometimes God is present neither to punish nor bless but instead to keep the universe existing and functioning the way he intended it to. In Christ, "all things hold together" (Col. 1:17). Christ is continually upholding "the universe by the word of his power" (Heb. 1:3).

God Is Spirit

Jesus affirmed that God is in no way limited to a spatial location when he said, "God is spirit" (John 4:24). God exists in such a way that his being is not made of any matter. He has no parts, no size, and no dimensions. He is unable to be perceived by our bodily senses. To think of his being in terms of anything else in the created universe would be a misrepresentation, for he is more excellent than any other kind of existence.

Yet God has chosen to make us, in our spiritual nature, somewhat like him in his spiritual nature. He has gifted us with spirits in which we are to worship him (John 4:24). Paul tells us those who are "joined to the Lord" become "one spirit with him" (1 Cor. 6:17). As one spirit with God, his Holy Spirit within us bears witness to our status as his adopted children

(Rom. 8:16). When we die, if we are joined with him, our spirit will return "to God who gave it" (Eccl. 12:7).

God Is Invisible

Because God is spirit, God is also invisible. "No one has ever seen God" (John 1:18). Nor will anyone ever be able to see God's total essence or all of his spiritual being.

The Bible does, however, record instances when people have seen outward manifestations of God. Isaiah tells us he "saw the Lord sitting upon a throne, high and lifted up" (Isa. 6:1). "The LORD appeared" to Abraham "by the oaks of Mamre" (Gen. 18:1). And Jacob said he saw "God face to face" (Gen. 32:30). In these and other similar instances, God took on a visible form to show himself to people. A much greater visible manifestation of God is found in the person of Jesus Christ. As Jesus said, "Whoever has seen me has seen the Father" (John 14:9).

Although no one can ever see God's total essence, which is invisible, God has at times chosen to show something of himself to people through visible, created things, and especially through the person of Jesus Christ.

God Is Omniscient

God "knows everything" (1 John 3:20). In one simple and eternal act, he fully knows himself and all actual and possible things. He knows all things that exist and all that happens. "No creature is hidden" from God's sight, "but all are naked and exposed to the eyes of him to whom we must give account" (Heb. 4:13). Since he fully knows himself (1 Cor. 2:10–11), he fully knows all things he could have done but did not do and all things he might have created but did not create. He also knows all possible events that will not actually happen, and events that would have resulted if some other events had turned out differently in history (see, for example, Matt. 11:21).

God is always, at all times, fully aware of everything, including everything that will happen. God himself affirms this in Isaiah 42:9: "New things I now declare; before they spring forth I tell you of them." He is the only One who has this full and complete knowledge of the future. "I am God, and there is no other; I am God, and there is none like me, declaring the end from the beginning and from ancient times things not yet done, saying, 'My counsel shall stand, and I will accomplish all my purpose'" (Isa. 46:9–10).

God's knowledge never changes or grows. Nothing surprises him; nothing is hidden from him. From all eternity God has known all things that would happen and all things that he would do. To claim anything less is to deny his omniscience.

God Is Wise

God is not only all-knowing but also all-wise. This means he always chooses the best possible goals and the best possible means to meet those goals. He is "the only wise God" (Rom. 16:27). He is "wise in heart" (Job 9:4) and with him "are wisdom and might; he has counsel and understanding" (Job 12:13).

His wisdom is manifest in many areas. For example, in his wisdom, he created all things (Ps. 104:24). His wisdom is also shown through the lives of "those who love God" and "those who are called according to his purpose." For those people, because of God's wisdom, "all things work together for good" (Rom. 8:28).

God gives this wisdom to his children. With this in mind, James encourages his readers, "If any of you lacks wisdom, let him ask God, who gives generously to all without reproach, and it will be given him" (James 1:5). Godly wisdom—the character quality found in living a life pleasing to him—is discovered through reading and obeying God's Word. "The testimony of the LORD is sure, making wise the simple" (Ps. 19:7).

Even so, we will never fully share God's wisdom. Because of the great "depth of the riches and wisdom and knowledge of God," his judgments are "unsearchable," and his ways are "inscrutable" (Rom. 11:33). At times he will allow us to understand the reasons things happen; at other times we will not be able to fully understand why things are the way they are or happened the way they did. During those difficult times, we must eventually "trust in the LORD" with "all" our heart and not lean on our "own understanding" (Prov. 3:5).

God Is Truthful

"The LORD is the true God" (Jer. 10:10). All his knowledge and all his words are both true and the final standard of truth. Once he says something, we can count on his doing it; we can count on him to be forever faithful to his promises (Num. 23:19). In fact, the essence of true faith is taking God at his word and relying on him to do as he promised.

We can imitate God's truthfulness in part by striving to have true knowledge of him and his Word. We can also imitate it by being truthful in what we say and do (Col. 3:9–10).

God Is Good

Jesus said, "No one is good except God alone" (Luke 18:19). Therefore, God is the final standard of good; all he is and does is good and worthy of approval. There is no higher standard of goodness than God's own character and his approval of whatever is consistent with that character. For example, his goodness and approval of goodness are seen through his creation: "God saw everything that he had made, and behold, it was very good" (Gen. 1:31).

Because God is the ultimate standard of goodness, he is also the ultimate source of all goodness. James tells us, "Every good gift and every perfect gift is from above, coming down from the Father of lights" (James 1:17). God is the one who bestows good gifts on his children. God promises not to withhold any good thing from "those who walk uprightly" (Ps. 84:11). Jesus confirms this when he says that God will "give good things to those who ask him" (Matt. 7:11). Even his discipline is a manifestation of his goodness and love (Heb. 12:10). Therefore, all the goodness that we seek is ultimately found in God himself. The psalmist realized this and wrote, "There is nothing on earth that I desire besides you" (Ps. 73:25).

God's goodness can often be seen through his mercy and grace. His mercy is his goodness toward those in misery and distress. His grace is his goodness toward those who deserve only punishment. Recipients of God's goodness—often received through his mercy and grace—are called to demonstrate that goodness to others. As Paul says in Galatians 6:10, "So then, as we have opportunity, let us do good to everyone, and especially to those who are of the household of faith."

God Is Love

As mentioned earlier, "God is love" (1 John 4:8). God eternally gives of himself for the good of others. Jesus tells us this self-giving attribute, God's love, was active "before the foundation of the world" (John 17:24). It was evident in the love that God the Father, God the Son, and God the Holy Spirit all had for each other (John 17:24; 14:31).

This eternal love finds its expression in God's self-giving love toward his children. John tells us, "In this is love, not that we have loved God but that he loved us and sent his Son to be the propitiation for our sins" (1 John 4:10). And Paul writes, "God shows his love for us in that while we were still sinners, Christ died for us" (Rom. 5:8).

Because God has loved and will love us for all eternity, we are able to give that love freely to others. In fact, Jesus summed up our responsibility to God when he said, "You shall love the Lord your God with all your heart and with all your soul and with all your mind. . . . And . . . you shall love your neighbor as yourself" (Matt. 22:37–39). And like God's love, our love is to be self-giving (1 John 3:16–17), not demonstrated in "word or talk but in deed and in truth" (1 John 3:18).

God Is Holy

"The LORD our God is holy" (Ps. 99:9). That means he is separated from sin and devoted to seeking his own honor. God is often called the "Holy One of Israel" (Ps. 71:22, for example). The seraphim (winged creatures) around his throne continually cry out, "Holy, holy, holy is the LORD of hosts" (Isa. 6:3).

God's holiness provides the pattern his children are to imitate. As he says in Leviticus 19:2, "You shall be holy, for I the LORD your God am holy." Through the power of the Holy Spirit, we are to "strive . . . for the holiness without which no one will see the Lord" (Heb. 12:14). The author of Hebrews tells us that God disciplines his children so that they "may share his holiness" (Heb. 12:10). As we are being made holy, individually and as members of the church (Eph. 5:26–27), we anticipate the day when all things in heaven and on earth will be separated from evil, purified from sin, and devoted solely to seeking God's honor with true moral purity (Zech. 14:20–21).

God Is Righteous and Just

Of God, Moses said, "All his ways are justice. A God of faithfulness and without iniquity, just and upright is he" (Deut. 32:4). As Moses said, God always acts in accordance with what is right, for he himself is the final standard of what is right. As judge of the world, he will do what is right (Gen. 18:25). He speaks the truth and declares "what is right" (Isa. 45:19). So, as we seek to do what is just and what is right—as we seek to bring about what ought to be—we must seek to do that which is in line with God's moral character, for that is the ultimate standard of righteousness.

Because God is righteous and just, he must treat people as they deserve. Therefore, he must punish that which is against him, that is, sin. However, sometimes God forgives people and does not punish them for their sin. How can he do that if he is just? God is able to forgive people because Christ died to take God's punishment for sin upon himself. In this way, Jesus demonstrated "God's righteousness, because in his divine forbearance he had passed over former sins. It was to show his righteousness at the present time, so that he might be just and the justifier of the one who has faith in Jesus" (Rom. 3:25–26).

Because God is all powerful, eventually all things will be made right. He will bring about justice. As ones who have benefited from his righteousness and justice, we are to join the Judge of the entire world in doing that which is right.

We should always seek to do what is right and to bring about justice on behalf of those who are not experiencing it. As Proverbs 21:3 tells us, "To do righteousness and justice is more acceptable to the LORD than sacrifice."

God Is Jealous

While explaining the first of the Ten Commandments, God says, "I the LORD your God am a jealous God" (Ex. 20:5). In his jealousy, God continually seeks to protect his own honor. He desires that worship be given only to himself and not to anyone or anything else. It is not wrong for God to continually seek his own honor, for it is an honor that only he, as God, deserves. That is why he can rightly say, "My glory I will not give to another" (Isa. 48:11).

God Is Wrathful toward Sin

God intensely hates all sin. God's wrath burns hot against sin, and it is this wrath that will eventually consume those who reject Jesus and continue in their sin. As Jesus said, "Whoever does not obey the Son shall not see life, but the wrath of God remains on him" (John 3:36). The "wrath of God," Paul says, "is revealed from heaven against all ungodliness and unrighteousness of men" (Rom. 1:18).

Therefore, wrath is an attribute for which we should thank and praise God. If God delighted in or was not troubled by sin, he wouldn't be a God worthy of our worship or praise. Sin is worthy of our hatred. In fact, we are encouraged by Christ's example to hate sin and wickedness (Heb. 1:9). Although we should not glory or rejoice at the demise of others but should love them and pray that they would repent of their evil deeds, it is also right to rejoice at the just punishment of evil actions. Ultimately, we should pray that evildoers would repent and trust Christ for forgiveness. In the case of those who trust Christ, God's wrath is satisfied because the just punishment fell on Christ at the cross (Rom. 3:25; 5:8–9). Thus, the wrath of God is not something those who believe in Jesus have any need to fear. The wrath that we deserved was fully given to Jesus, who through his death and resurrection, "delivers us from the wrath to come" (1 Thess. 1:10). But for those who reject Jesus, God's wrath is something to fear, for it fully remains on them (John 3:36).

God Wills What He Will

God continually "works all things according to the counsel of his will" (Eph. 1:11). God's will is the ultimate reason for everything that happens. It is the way God approves and determines to bring about every action necessary for the existence of and activity of himself and all his creation. God's will is how he chooses to do what he does and doesn't do.

For example, all things were created by God's will (Rev. 4:11), human governments have their power according to God's will (Rom. 13:1), and sometimes it is God's will that his children suffer (1 Peter 3:17). All the events of our life are subject to God's will. That is why James encourages us not to say we will do this or that, but instead say, "If the Lord wills, we will live and do this or that" (James 4:15).

Even the death of Christ and all the events surrounding it took place according to God's will. Luke tells us in Acts 4:27–28, those who were involved in Christ's death did whatever God's hand and plan "had predestined to take place."

Sometimes God's will is clearly revealed, such as when, from Scripture, we clearly know what we should do or what God has specifically commanded us to do. This is what Jesus was referring to when he told us to pray, "Your will be done, on earth as it is in heaven" (Matt. 6:10).

At other times, Scripture does not give us clear direction as to what we are to do or how we are to act. It's at times like these that our attitude should be one of humble reliance on God and his sovereign control over the events in our lives. We should plan our steps, as James encouraged us to, by saying "If the Lord wills, we will live and do this or that" (James 4:15).

Therefore, we must exhibit much caution, especially in the midst of difficult situations, in saying with any degree of certainty what the Lord's will is if it isn't clear from Scripture. For example, there is a danger in speaking of evil events as happening according to the will of God even though we may find places where the Bible speaks this way. When we explain evil as the result of God's will, it can sound as if God is to be blamed for evil and sin or as if God delights in such evil. But this is not the case. In the Bible, human beings and sinful angels (demons) are always blamed for evil, sinful actions, and God is never blamed. Even the death of Christ, which the Bible clearly states happened "according to the definite plan and foreknowledge of God," was carried out "by the hands of lawless men" (Acts 2:23).

God is not to be blamed for, or thought responsible for, sinful or evil things. The exact relationship between his will and evil is not something he has chosen to completely reveal to us. Therefore, we must take comfort in the fact that "the secret things belong to the LORD our God" (Deut. 29:29).

God Has Freedom

Psalm 115:3 says, "Our God is in the heavens; he does all that he pleases." Nothing can hinder God from doing his will. He is not constrained by anything outside of himself; he is completely free to do whatever he wants to do. He is not under any authority or restraint; no person or force can ever dictate what he should or will do.

Although we can imitate God in his freedom when we exercise our will and make choices, all those choices are ultimately subject to God's will. As Proverbs 16:9 tells us, "The heart of man plans his way, but the LORD establishes his steps." Even "the king's heart is a stream of water in the hand of the LORD; he turns it wherever he will" (Prov. 21:1).

God Is Omnipotent

"Is anything too hard for the LORD?" asks Genesis 18:14. Although the question is answered many times throughout the Bible, one clear answer is found when Jeremiah says to God, "Nothing is too hard for you" (Jer. 32:17).

God is omnipotent. He is all powerful. He is able to do all his holy will. There are no limits on what he decides to do. He "is able," Paul tells us, "to do far more abundantly than all that we ask or think" (Eph. 3:20). As Jesus says, "With God all things are possible" (Matt. 19:26). God's power is infinite.

But there are some things God cannot do. He can neither will nor do anything that denies his own character. For example, he cannot lie (Titus 1:2), he cannot be tempted with evil (James 1:13), and he cannot deny himself (2 Tim. 2:13). Therefore, God's use of his infinite power is qualified by his other attributes.

As we imitate God by utilizing the limited power he has given us to accomplish the things he desires us to do, we show a faint reflection of his infinite power, and thus we bring him glory.

God Is Perfect

Jesus tells us in Matthew 5:48, "Your heavenly Father is perfect." This means God fully possesses all excellent qualities and lacks no part of any qualities that would be desirable for him. We can imitate his perfection by striving to "be perfect," as Jesus commanded us to do in the same verse. Although we won't attain the perfection we often desire here on earth, through the work of Christ on our behalf we can continually make progress toward that perfection throughout our lives.

God Is Blessed

God's blessedness means that he fully delights in himself and in all that reflects his character. He himself is the focus of all happiness and delight; therefore, his complete fullness of joy is found in himself.

But God also chooses to delight in his creation. When he saw what he made, he said it was "very good" (Gen. 1:31), indicating his delight in what he had made. God longs to rejoice over his children, "as the bridegroom rejoices over the bride" (Isa. 62:5).

As we find delight and happiness in what is pleasing to God—be it the work of others, aspects of our own lives, or things of creation—we demonstrate the ways God has blessed us and therefore honor him and imitate him in his blessedness. We find our greatest blessedness and ultimate happiness in the source of all good things—God himself.

God Is Beautiful

In Psalm 27:4 David tells us that his single great longing in life is to dwell in God's house for his entire life. One reason he gives for this longing is that he desires to "gaze upon the beauty of the LORD." God is the sum of all desirable qualities, and he possesses every quality that is truly desirable. Therefore, as David discovered, all our longings and all our desires will only ultimately find their fulfillment in God, the only One who is truly beautiful.

God Is a Unity

Although some of God's attributes may seem to be emphasized more than others, it is important to realize that God is unified in all his attributes. He is not more of one attribute than another. He is not divided into parts, and he is not one attribute at one point in history and another attribute at another time. He is fully and completely every attribute (even those not mentioned here) at every time.

Scripture never singles out one of God's attributes as more important than the rest. For example, "God is light" (1 John 1:5) and "God is love" (1 John 4:8). He is not part light and part love; he is not love during the day and light at night. He is, at all times and in all ways, both light and love. Each one of God's attributes qualifies each other attribute.

Each of God's attributes represents one aspect of his character; each provides us with a perspective on who he is. And each also provides us with some perspective on who he has made us to be.

Questions for Review and Application

1. What are some attributes that God most clearly shares with us? What are some attributes he doesn't share very much with us? Name one attribute of God that you would like to imitate more fully in your daily life, and tell why.
2. Can you tell what some of the dangers would be in considering one of God's attributes more important than all the others?
3. Which of God's attributes seems most amazing to you? What have you learned about God through this attribute?

chapter 3

WHAT IS THE TRINITY?

Sometimes people use three different names when referring to God: God or Father, Jesus Christ, and the Holy Spirit. But these are more than simply different names for one person; they are, in fact, the names of three very distinct persons. But even though God the Father, God the Son (Jesus), and God the Holy Spirit have eternally existed as three distinct persons, there is only one God. This is called the doctrine of the Trinity. The idea of three persons and only one God is difficult to understand completely. Even so, it is one of the most important ideas of the Christian faith.

The Bible's View of the Trinity

The word *trinity* is never found in the Bible, but the idea represented by the word is affirmed in many places. For instance, in Genesis 1:26 God said, "Let us make man in our image, after our likeness." His use of "us" and "our" implies that more than one person was involved in creation. The only other beings that God could possibly be referring to are angels, but we are not made in the image of angels but "in the image of God" (Gen. 1:27), so this verse must imply that there is more than one person in God.

When Jesus was baptized, "the heavens were opened to

him, and he saw the Spirit of God descending like a dove and coming to rest on him; and . . . a voice from heaven said, 'This is my beloved Son, with whom I am well pleased'" (Matt. 3:16–17). At this moment all three members of the Trinity were performing three distinct activities: God the Father was speaking, God the Son was being baptized, and God the Holy Spirit was resting on the Son.

Similarly, when Jesus sent his disciples out to do their work, he commanded them to "make disciples of all nations, baptizing them in the name of the Father and of the Son and of the Holy Spirit" (Matt. 28:19). In saying this, Jesus is affirming that all three members of the Trinity are distinct in their personhood (the Father can't be the Son, for example). Jude 20–21 also affirms the three distinct persons in the Trinity: "Praying in the Holy Spirit, keep yourselves in the love of God, waiting for the mercy of our Lord Jesus Christ."

The Meaning of the Trinity

Because God is three distinct persons, the Father is not the Son or the Holy Spirit, the Son is not the Father or the Holy Spirit, and the Holy Spirit is not the Father or the Son. This was demonstrated through a number of passages above.

Each of the persons of the Trinity is fully God. God the Father's deity is shown from the first verse of the Bible— "In the beginning, God created the heavens and the earth" (Gen. 1:1)—and throughout the pages of Scripture. When the Bible refers simply to God, more often than not it is referring to God the Father.

But God the Son, who came to earth as Jesus Christ, is also fully God. As Paul writes of Jesus in Colossians 2:9, "In him the whole fullness of deity dwells bodily." Therefore, Jesus' disciple Thomas was correct when he said to Jesus, "My Lord and my God!" (John 20:28). In fact, John said he wrote his gospel so that people would "believe that Jesus is the Christ, the Son of God" (John 20:31).

Finally, God the Holy Spirit is also fully God. Because both the Father and Son are God, it makes sense that all three are mentioned with equal importance in passages like Matthew 28:19 ("baptizing them in the name of the Father and of the Son and of the Holy Spirit"). This indicates that Scripture views all three as fully God. Peter confirms this view when he accuses someone of lying "to the Holy Spirit" (Acts 5:3) and then further explains that this man has "not lied to man but to God" (v. 4). The Spirit, Paul says, is omniscient like God the Father: "No one comprehends the thoughts of God except the Spirit of God" (1 Cor. 2:11).

But the Bible is also clear that there is only one God and not three. The Bible says that God is only one essence or one being. Deuteronomy 6:4 says, "The LORD is one." God frequently echoes this statement when he speaks, making it clear that there is no other God but him. Isaiah 45:5 is one example of this: "I am the LORD, and there is no other, besides me there is no God."

Paul affirms this in Romans 3:30 when he writes, "God is one" and again in 1 Timothy 2:5 when he writes, "There is one God." In James 2:19 we find that even the demons acknowledge this: "You believe that God is one; you do well. Even the demons believe—and shudder!"

At times it can seem difficult to understand how there are three distinct persons of the Trinity, each with the whole being of God in himself, even though there is only one God, and he is undivided. And it should be difficult. The Trinity is one of those mysteries we can only describe in part. Although different analogies from creation can help us a bit in understanding the Trinity, ultimately all analogies fail in describing this mystery, for they attempt to explain the being of God in terms of the creation. They are attempts to explain how God is like the creation. But nothing in creation is exactly like God's being. Attempts to simplify or fully explain this mystery all fail and often lead to beliefs that are contrary to the Bible's teachings. In short, the doctrine of the Trinity is something we will never fully understand, for parts of it are beyond our comprehension. It is, in part, one of those "secret things" that "belong to the LORD our God" (Deut. 29:29).

Yet it is extremely important that this mystery be true. For example, if Jesus is not both fully God and a separate person from God, then he could not have borne the complete wrath of God, died, and risen from the dead. And if Jesus didn't rise from the dead, any belief in him is foolish, and those who claim to be Christians are, in the words of Paul, "of all people most to be pitied" (1 Cor. 15:19).

The Distinct Roles of the Trinity

All three members of the Trinity have different roles. For example, in creation we know that God spoke the earth into being (Gen. 1:9–10). But John 1:3 tells us that God the Son carried out those words: "All things were made through him, and without him was not any thing made that was made." And, as Genesis 1:2 tells us, while God was creating, "the Spirit of God was hovering over the face of the waters," that is, sustaining and manifesting God's presence in creation.

Different roles within the Trinity can also be seen in our salvation. God the Father "so loved the world, that he gave his only Son," whom he sent "into the world . . . in order that the world might be saved through him" (John 3:16–17). Of his role, Jesus said, "I have come down from heaven, not to do my own will but the will of him who sent me" (John 6:38). And that will was that Jesus die for our sins so that we didn't have to (Heb. 10:10). When Jesus rose from the dead and ascended into heaven, he and the Father sent the Holy Spirit to bring completion to the work the Father and the Son had started (John 14:26; 16:7).

In both creation and redemption, the Father, the Son, and the Spirit all had distinct roles. It was the Father who directed and sent both the Son and the Spirit. And it was the Son who, along with the Father, sent the Spirit. The Son was obedient to the Father, and the Spirit was obedient to both the Father and the Son. And while both the Son and the Spirit have and continue to carry out their roles in equal deity with the Father, they do so in submission to the Father.

These different functions and roles are simply the out-working of the eternal relationship between the Father, Son, and Spirit. They do not diminish the deity, attributes, or essential nature of the Father, Son, or Spirit. The distinction is simply in the ways they relate to each other and to the creation. This is far different from our own experience where every person is a different being as well. But somehow God's being is so different from ours that it can be both undivided and can unfold itself into interpersonal relationships among three distinct persons. This is far different from anything we have ever experienced, will experience, or can fully understand.

Yet the unity and diversity within the Trinity provide a wonderful basis for the unity and diversity we experience in everyday life. In marriage, for example, two distinct persons come together, and through marriage they become "one flesh" (Eph. 5:31). As husband and wife they have equal standing, value, and personhood before God, but they also have distinct roles. Just as the Father has authority over the Son, so in marriage the husband has authority over the wife. As Paul says in 1 Corinthians 11:3, "The head of every man is Christ, the head of a wife is her husband, and the head of Christ is God" (see also Eph. 5:22–25; Col. 3:18–19; 1 Peter 3:1–7). Even though it may be difficult at times to figure out just how the roles of husband and wife are to be specifically defined, the Bible makes it clear that the relationship within the Trinity provides the model for the relationship of marriage.

Another example of unity and diversity is seen in the church, which has "many members" all with different skills and gifts but "one body" with one purpose (1 Cor. 12:12). The church also includes members "from every nation, from all tribes and peoples and languages" (Rev. 7:9). This diversity adds a complexity that shows us the wisdom of God in allowing both unity and diversity to exist within his world. The unity and diversity that exists in this world is simply a reflection of the unity and diversity that exists within the Trinity.

Questions for Review and Application

1. Can you name three or four key passages of Scripture that tell us about the Trinity? What exactly do these passages tell us about the Trinity?
2. Why do all analogies fail in their ability to fully explain the Trinity? Does this mean we should try to come up with an analogy that works? Why or why not?
3. How do the different ways the Father, Son, and Holy Spirit relate to each other provide us with a model for the ways we are to relate to each other?

chapter 4

WHAT IS CREATION?

Where did the universe come from? And what is its purpose? Should we think of the creation as good or as evil? In this chapter we seek to understand how God created the universe, what kind of universe he created, and how we should think of the creation today.

The Created Creation

God created the universe out of nothing; nothing but God existed before the universe was created. All things—what Genesis 1:1 calls "the heavens and the earth"—were created by God. John 1:3 affirms this: "All things were made through him." And in Colossians 1:16 we read, "By him all things were created, in heaven and on earth, visible and invisible." And as we saw in chapter 3, all the members of the Trinity were involved in this process.

God spoke all of creation into existence—from land and waters to plants and animals (Gen. 1:3–25)—that is, all of creation except for man. Both man and woman were created by God's very hands and received life from God's very breath (Gen. 2:7, 22). This intimate, special creation is one sign of the special place God designed human beings to have within his creation. In addition, human beings are the only ones that God made "in his own image" (Gen. 1:27). To be in God's image means to be like God and to represent God. As God's image, man is the pinnacle of all creation, more like God than any other creature, and the only one appointed to rule over the rest of creation as God's representative (Gen. 1:28–31).

Many scientific theories directly conflict with a biblical view of creation, such as the theory that all living things came into being as a result of random mutations over a long period of time, rather than as a result of God's intelligent design and infinite power. Scientific theories that do not see God as the Creator fail to give us the dignity that is given by the biblical account. The Bible teaches that although God did not need to create anything, he chose to create us and chose to create us in his image.

On the other hand, sometimes scientific observations of the world can correct people's misunderstandings. At one time many Christians thought that the Bible taught that the sun goes around the earth. They opposed the theories of Galileo, whose astronomical observations led him to believe that the earth rotates and also orbits the sun. Eventually the whole church recognized that the Bible never teaches that the sun goes around the earth, so they could accept Galileo's observations. We should exercise care, then, in speaking to issues that the Bible does not clearly speak to. And when our observations of the natural world seem to conflict with our understanding of Scripture, we should look again at both, seeking to find where our limited understanding and imperfect knowledge of either could be wrong. Ultimately, a proper understanding of science and a proper understanding of Scripture will not be in conflict.

The Bible is clear: God created the earth and all that is in

and on it from nothing. He created man from the dust of the
world he created. Before creation nothing existed but God.
Therefore, nothing but God is eternal. Nothing but God can
ultimately rule over that which he made. And so nothing but
God is worthy of our worship. Because we are special products
of God's creation, this fact should create great humility in us.
In addition, because God created the universe from nothing,
and because he didn't need to create it, he must have created
it for some purpose. Because we are special products of God's
creation, this should give us great dignity.

The Distinct but Dependent Creation

As Creator, God is distinct from his creation. He is not part of
the creation. He is unlike his creation in many ways. He made
all things and rules over all things. He is greater than creation
and very much independent of it. He doesn't need creation in
any way.

But God is also intimately involved in creation. With his
very breath he gave life to his very own image. "In his hand
is the life of every living thing and the breath of all mankind"
(Job 12:10). God himself "gives to all mankind life and breath
and everything," and "in him we live and move and have our
being" (Acts 17:25, 28). We are, Paul says, "God's offspring"
(Acts 17:29).

God is both involved in and distinct from creation. He is
not dependent on creation, but creation is dependent on him.
Therefore, nothing in creation is worthy of the affection that
God deserves. Although God is greater than creation, he did
not choose to leave creation to function on its own. Instead, he
chose to stay intimately involved with his creation, especially
those made in his image. Therefore, he is not so removed from

us that he cannot or will not be intimately involved in our lives and our struggles. He is near; he is "our refuge and strength, a very present help in trouble" (Ps. 46:1). Because God is greater than all creation and involved with all creation, if we hope in God, we have nothing to fear.

The Glory-Giving Creation

All of creation was made to give glory to God. "The heavens declare the glory of God, and the sky above proclaims his handiwork" (Ps. 19:1). God says we were also created for his glory (Isa. 43:7). In fact, God's role as Creator makes him worthy of our glory: "Worthy are you, our Lord and God, to receive glory and honor and power, for you created all things, and by your will they existed and were created" (Rev. 4:11).

God's creation shows his superior power and wisdom. "It is he who made the earth by his power, who established the world by his wisdom, and by his understanding stretched out the heavens" (Jer. 10:12). Even a brief reflection on the complexity, diversity, and beauty in creation should cause us to praise God for his power, wisdom, and understanding.

God did not need any more glory from creation. All the glory God needs has been forever within the Trinity. Instead, the Bible is clear: God "created all things," and by his will "they existed and were created" (Rev. 4:11). Creation was a totally free act of God. He created the universe to show his greatness, to demonstrate his excellence, and to delight in his work. Therefore, as we take spontaneous delight in God's creative activities, our creative activities, and the creative activities of others, we are giving glory to God by imitating the delight he takes in his creation.

The Good Creation

God can delight in his creation because it gives him glory. He also delights in it because, as Genesis 1:31 tells us, when God looked over "everything that he had made," he considered it "very good." Even though the creation doesn't always function as it is supposed to because of sin, we should also consider the material creation good. "For everything created by God is good, and nothing is to be rejected if it is received with thanksgiving" (1 Tim. 4:4).

Thus, we are to enjoy the good things God has created for us. Although some things in creation can be used for sinful purposes, their potentially harmful use does not make them evil in all situations. For example, although Paul says, "the love of money is a root of all kinds of evils" (1 Tim. 6:10), he also says that God himself "richly provides us with everything to enjoy" (1 Tim. 6:17). Therefore, we should joyfully use the abundant earth God has given us and seek to develop it in a way that brings glory and honor to God's name.

Questions for Review and Application

1. In what ways do God's acts of creation give us great humility? How do they give us great dignity?
2. List some of the ways the earth, the animals, and you yourself can give glory to God the Creator.
3. What does God think about all of his creation? How did his view of the creation change after Adam and Eve sinned? How is God's view of all his creation different from your view of specific aspects of his creation?

chapter **5**

WHAT IS PRAYER?

One of the ways God allows his creation to stay involved with him is through prayer. Prayer, which is personal communication from us to God, not only helps us know *about* God but also helps us truly *know* God. Through prayer we can communicate our requests to God, confess our sins to God, and give adoration, praise, and thanksgiving to God.

The Reason for Prayer

God does not want us to pray so that he can find out what we need, for Jesus said, "Your Father knows what you need before you ask him" (Matt. 6:8). Instead, God wants us to pray so that our dependence on him can increase. When we come to him in prayer about something, we express a trust in him, a trust that he will hear and answer our prayers. That is why Jesus compared our prayers to a child asking his father for a fish or an egg (Luke 11:9–12). As a child trusts and expects his father to provide for him, so we ought to expect, in faith, that God will provide for us. Jesus said, "Whatever you ask in prayer, you will receive, if you have faith" (Matt. 21:22).

God does not just desire that our trust in him will grow through prayer; he also desires that our love for him and our relationship with him will deepen and grow. When we truly pray, we pray with the wholeness of our character, relating to the wholeness of his character. Therefore, what we think and feel about God will come through in our prayers. This will, in turn, deepen our love and understanding of God and, in the end, deepen our relationship with him. This is something that God delights in. It is also something that brings him glory.

Finally, God wants us to pray because it allows us to be a part of a story that is greater than our own. It allows us to be involved in activities that have eternal significance. When we pray, God's kingdom is advanced as his will is done "on earth as it is in heaven" (Matt. 6:10).

The Effectiveness of Prayer

When we ask for things in prayer, God often responds to those prayers. Jesus makes this clear when he says, "Ask, and it will be given to you; seek, and you will find; knock, and it will be opened to you. For everyone who asks receives, and the one who seeks finds, and to the one who knocks it will be opened" (Luke 11:9–10). Our failure to ask God for things is often the reason we do not receive what he delights to give to us. James says, "You do not have, because you do not ask" (James 4:2). The Scriptures give many examples of God responding, even changing the way he acts, in response to the prayers of individuals. For example, when the Lord told Moses he would destroy the people of Israel for their sin, Moses responded with the following prayer: "Turn from your burning anger and relent from this disaster against your people" (Ex. 32:12). In response, "the LORD relented from the disaster that he had spoken of bringing on his people" (Ex. 32:14). On a more personal level, John tells us that "if we confess our sins, he is faithful and just to forgive us our sins and to cleanse us from all unrighteousness" (1 John 1:9). These two examples, along with the many others in the Bible, should encourage us to pray more, boldly asking the Lord to work in ways only he can work.

On our own, though, we have no right to boldly ask God for anything. Our own personal sin should disqualify us from requesting anything from a holy God. But if our faith is in Jesus, the Bible tells us he is the reason our prayers are effective. He stands as the "one mediator between God and men" (1 Tim. 2:5). Or, as Jesus said, "No one comes to the Father except through me" (John 14:6). Therefore, God is under no obligation to answer the prayers of those who have rejected his Son. Although he is aware of such prayers and at times out of his mercy chooses to answer them, he does not promise to hear and answer the prayers of unbelievers as he does the prayers of believers that are in accordance with his will.

Because Jesus is the only true mediator between a holy God and sinful men, he could tell his disciples, "Whatever you ask of the Father in my name, he will give it to you" (John 16:23). When he said this, Jesus did not mean that we must tack the phrase "in Jesus' name" onto every one of our prayers. Instead, he meant that our prayers should be prayed based on his authority as our mediator and in accordance with his character. This is, in part, what John meant when he wrote to those "who believe in the name of the Son of God" and said, "If we ask anything according to his will he hears us" (1 John 5:13–14).

Our Attitude in Prayer

Not only does he hear us, John says, but "if we know that he hears us in whatever we ask, we know that we have the requests that we have asked of him" (1 John 5:15). These effective prayers that Jesus answers and we so long to pray must be prayed "according to his will" (1 John 5:14). Praying according to God's will often requires humility on our part, for it requires that we pray not simply for what we desire but instead for what God desires.

Sometimes it is easy to know what God's will is and, therefore, to pray in accordance with his will. For example, if we pray in line with a direct command or declaration of his will in Scripture, then we will be asking God to do what he desires to do and asking for things that please him. In fact, Jesus encourages us to have God's very words within us as we pray: "If you abide in me, and my words abide in you, ask whatever you wish, and it will be done for you" (John 15:7).

There are, however, many situations where it isn't abundantly clear what God's will is. At these times, we should pray in line with the general principles of Scripture, asking God to work on our behalf and telling him the requests that seem best to us as far as we understand them. We should do so with a humble attitude, realizing that we are asking God to work only if it is in line with his will. Sometimes God will grant what we ask. At other times he will deepen our understanding of the situation so that our hearts are moved to ask for something else. And at other times he will seem to be silent. At those difficult times we should be content to know that God's will in this situation is even better than immediately receiving what we have asked.

Even so, Jesus encourages us to pray in such a way that we believe we have already received (that is, God has already decided to give us) what we ask for (Mark 11:24). This kind of faith is not something we can create or force if we don't really believe; it is a gift from God that he often gives in the midst of prayer. This "assurance of things hoped for" and "conviction of things not seen" (Heb. 11:1) comes from a belief that

God exists and "that he rewards those who seek him" (Heb. 11:6). Anything in our lives that displeases God will hinder our prayers.

As the psalmist explains, "If I had cherished iniquity in my heart, the Lord would not have listened" (Ps. 66:18). Similarly, "The LORD is far from the wicked, but he hears the prayer of the righteous" (Prov. 15:29). And "The eyes of the Lord are on the righteous, and his ears are open to their prayer. But the face of the Lord is against those who do evil" (1 Peter 3:12).

However, we do not need to be completely free from sin in order for God to hear our prayers. If God only answered the prayers of perfect, sinless people, then God would only answer the prayers of Jesus. And, as was said earlier, it is only because of Jesus' work on our behalf that God will hear our prayers. We do, however, need to seek holiness in our lives, for this is often the path to greater blessing.

When we do sin, God urges us to use his gift of prayer to seek his forgiveness. Confessing our sins to God restores our day-to-day relationship with him. When we confess our sins, God is "faithful and just" to forgive those sins and not punish us for them (1 John 1:9), because Christ was already punished for them on the cross. With this encouragement we should not only seek the Lord's forgiveness for the wrong we know we have done, but we should also ask that he declare us "innocent from hidden faults" (Ps. 19:12). In addition, James encourages us to confess our sins "to one another" and to "pray for one another" so that we may be healed (James 5:16).

Finally, in light of God's work on our behalf, we should ask for things with a humble attitude, for "God opposes the proud, but gives grace to the humble" (James 4:6). This means, in part, that we realize we will not always ask for things as we ought or in accordance with God's will. And therefore, sometimes our prayers won't be answered as we desire them to be answered.

When our prayers aren't answered, we join the company of men like Jesus and Paul whose prayers were not answered. Even Jesus, before he was crucified, asked his Father to "remove this cup" from him. But his humility and submission to God's will are evident in the second part of his prayer: "Nevertheless, not my will, but yours, be done" (Luke 22:42).

"Three times" Paul "pleaded with the Lord" to take away his affliction; the Lord did not do so, but instead told Paul, "My grace is sufficient for you, for my power is made perfect in weakness" (2 Cor. 12:8–9). These unanswered prayers did not deter either Jesus' or Paul's trust in a God who works "all things . . . together for good" (Rom. 8:28). God still promises us today, "I will never leave you nor forsake you" (Heb. 13:5). Therefore, regardless of the situation, we can confidently say, "The Lord is my helper; I will not fear; what can man do to me?" (Heb. 13:6).

Questions for Review and Application

1. Why does God want us to pray? How have you recently experienced these benefits of prayer? Take a moment to pray, thanking God for how he has blessed you through prayer.
2. Is God required to give us what we ask for in prayer? Why or why not?
3. Is there anything in your life right now that might be hindering your prayers? If so, take a moment to pray, asking God to forgive you of those things that hinder your prayers.

chapter 6

WHAT ARE ANGELS, SATAN, AND DEMONS?

Up to this point, when discussing God's creation, we have limited our discussion to the physical realm. But there are also spiritual creatures God has created called angels (and fallen angels called demons; Satan is considered the head of the demons).

Angels

Angels are created spiritual beings with moral judgment and high intelligence but without physical bodies. They are God's warriors and as a group are often referred to as the host (or armies) of heaven. They have not always existed; they are part of the universe God created. Ezra affirms this when he says of God, "You have made heaven, the heaven of heavens, with all their host" (Neh. 9:6).

Since angels are "spirits" (Heb. 1:14), they do not have physical bodies, for as Jesus says, "A spirit does not have flesh and bones" (Luke 24:39). Therefore, angels cannot ordinarily be seen unless the Lord opens our eyes (as he did with Balaam in Numbers 22:31) or they take on bodily form to appear to us (as happened at Jesus' tomb in Matthew 28:5). Normally, though, angels are invisible as they perform their ordinary activities of guarding us in all our ways (Ps. 91:11) and joining us in our worship of God (Heb. 12:22). Angels demonstrated moral judgment when "they sinned" and were cast out of heaven (2 Peter 2:4). They demonstrate their intelligence through speaking to humans (see Matt. 28:5, for example) and singing praise to God (see Rev. 4:11, for example).

Angels have great power. They are called "mighty ones" (Ps. 103:20) and are "greater in might and power" than unrighteous humans (2 Peter 2:11). Even so, God demonstrates a greater love for humans than for angels, for "God did not spare angels when they sinned, but cast them into hell and committed them to chains of gloomy darkness" (2 Peter 2:4). In contrast, when Adam and Eve sinned, though they were cast out of their paradise, they were not cast into hell. And instead of putting them in chains, God made clothes for them, covering their shame (Gen. 3:21–23).

As angels obediently carry out God's plans by doing "his word" (Ps. 103:20), they serve as examples for us. They also serve as examples for us as they worship and glorify God continually (see Rev. 5:11–12, for example). We should, therefore, be aware of the unseen presence of angels as we go about our daily lives. They may be joining us in worship, protecting and guarding us, or even visiting us as strangers seeking hospitality (Heb. 13:2). But we are not to pray to or worship angels. When John tried to worship an angel, the angel quickly said, "You must not do that! I am a fellow servant with you and your brothers who hold to the testimony of Jesus" (Rev. 19:10). We are to worship God and pray to God; we are not to treat angels, which are part of God's creation, the same way we would treat God.

Demons

Demons are evil angels who sinned against God and who now continually work evil in the world. They are the angels whom God "did not spare . . . when they sinned, but cast them into hell and committed them to chains of gloomy darkness" (2 Peter 2:4). But demons did not start out as evil. As part of the original creation, they were part of the "everything" God made, that he considered "very good" (Gen. 1:31). Although the Bible does not tell us specifically when they fell, sometime between their creation and Satan's tempting of Eve to sin, these demons "did not stay within their own position of authority, but left their proper dwelling" (Jude 6) and were cast into hell.

Satan is the personal name of the head of the demons. He is mentioned by name in passages like 1 Chronicles 21:1, where it says, "Satan stood against Israel and incited David to number Israel." Jesus speaks directly to him when tempted in the wilderness: "Be gone, Satan!" (Matt. 4:10). When the disciples tell Jesus that the demons are subject to his name, Jesus responds by saying, "I saw Satan fall like lightning from heaven" (Luke 10:18). The Bible also uses the following names for Satan: "the devil" (Matt. 4:1), "the serpent" (Gen. 3:1), "Beelzebul" (Matt. 10:25), "the ruler of this world" (John 12:31), "the prince of the power of the air" (Eph. 2:2), and "the evil one" (Matt. 13:19).

Satan was a "murderer from the beginning" and the "father of lies" (John 8:44). "The devil," 1 John 3:8 tells us, "has been sinning from the beginning." He is the originator of sin, having sinned before he "deceived Eve by his cunning" (2 Cor. 11:3). He also tried to tempt Christ to sin (Matt. 4:1–11) so that Jesus would fail in his mission "to destroy the works of the devil" (1 John 3:8). Satan and his demons will try to use every type of destructive tactic to blind people "from seeing the light of the gospel of the glory of Christ" (2 Cor. 4:4). They will also use similar destructive tactics—such as temptation, doubt, lies, murder, guilt, fear, confusion, sickness, envy, pride, and slander—to hinder a Christian's witness and usefulness.

The devil and his demons are limited both in their own power and by God's control in what they can and can't do. They are kept in "eternal chains under gloomy darkness" (Jude 6). Satan himself can be successfully resisted through the authority of Christ: "Resist the devil, and he will flee from you" (James 4:7). Satan and his demons cannot know the future, for only God can declare "the end from the beginning and from ancient times things not yet done" (Isa. 46:10). Although they may be able to observe what we do on a daily basis (and from this draw conclusions about our thoughts or our future), they cannot know for certain what we are thinking or what our future holds (see Dan. 2:27–28, where no one speaking by any other power than the God of heaven could know the king's dream).

Demonic Activity

Like God's angels, Satan and his demons are active in the world today, and they work much evil. But they are not solely responsible for all the evil in the world. Much of the sin mentioned in the Bible is not the result of Satan or his demons but instead the result of an individual person's own actions (James 1:14). Nevertheless, the Bible encourages us to "be sober-minded" and "watchful," for "the devil prowls around like a roaring lion, seeking someone to devour" (1 Peter 5:8). Therefore, we are encouraged to "resist him" (1 Peter 5:9) and "give no opportunity to the devil" (Eph. 4:27).

As these attacks from Satan and his demons come in various forms and to various degrees, those who believe in Jesus should realize that through death, Jesus nullified the power of "the one who has the power of death, that is, the devil" (Heb. 2:14). And at the cross God "disarmed the rulers and authorities and put them to open shame, by triumphing over them" in Christ (Col. 2:15). Therefore, if Satan or his demons mount an attack against us, we should take confidence in Christ's victory and use "the weapons of our warfare" that "have divine power to destroy strongholds" (2 Cor. 10:4). At times we may also decide to speak directly to an evil spirit, commanding it to leave in the name of Jesus (see Luke 9:1; 10:17; Acts 8:7; 16:18; James 4:7). We should not fear demons, for "he who is in you is greater than he who is in the world" (1 John 4:4). All the time we should "not rejoice . . . that the spirits are subject" to us but instead "rejoice" that our "names are written in heaven" (Luke 10:20).

In Romans 16:20 Paul tells Christians, "The God of peace will soon crush Satan under your feet." As the good news of the gospel is preached and people come to believe in Jesus, another spiritual battle is won. And someday Christ will come and completely remove the influence of Satan and demons from this world (see 2 Thess. 2:8; Rev. 20:1–3).

Questions for Review and Application

1. How are the angels like us? How are they different from us?
2. What is the primary role of angels in the world today?
3. What are some of the things that the Bible tells us about Satan? How do these things put you on guard against Satan? How do these things remove some fears you may have about Satan?

chapter 7

WHAT IS MAN?

After God created the plants and animals on the earth, he had one more thing to create, the pinnacle of his creation:

> So God created man in his own image, in the image of God he created him; male and female he created them. And God blessed them. And God said to them, "Be fruitful and multiply and fill the earth and subdue it and have dominion over the fish of the sea and over the birds of the heavens and over every living thing that moves on the earth." (Genesis 1:27–28)

God did not create us because he was lacking or needing anything. He wasn't lonely, nor did he need someone or something to bring him praise or give him glory. But he still chose to create us, and we do bring him glory. In Isaiah 43:7, God says, "Everyone who is called by my name . . . I created for my glory." Although this fact is supposed to give our lives significance, unless we understand what it means, it can seem empty and meaningless. To give God glory means to give him great honor and praise, and we can do that in various ways.

Created for God's Glory

Because we were created for God's glory, our ultimate goal in life should be to live for his glory. Giving God glory will give our lives purpose and meaning; it will give us the joy in our life that we all long for. Giving God glory is part of the life Jesus spoke of when he said, "I came that they may have life and have it abundantly" (John 10:10).

One of the ways we glorify God is by enjoying him. As David says, "In your presence there is fullness of joy; at your right hand are pleasures forevermore" (Ps. 16:11). Fullness of joy is found in knowing God and delighting in him. When we do this, we give him the glory that he desires and that we long to give to him. In the midst of this, we find God rejoicing over us "with gladness" and exulting over us "with loud singing" (Zeph. 3:17).

Created in God's Image

If all the Bible told us about ourselves is that we were created for God's glory, this would be a wonderful thing, but it wouldn't really distinguish us much from the rest of creation. For, "the heavens declare the glory of God, and the sky above proclaims his handiwork" (Ps. 19:1). Part of our uniqueness, however, comes from the fact that we are the only part of God's creation made "in the image of God" (Gen. 1:27).

As creatures made in God's image, we were made to be like him. Therefore, the more we understand about God, the more we understand about ourselves. And the more we understand about ourselves, the more we understand about God. For example, we are moral creatures, created with an innate sense of right and wrong. This is a reflection of God's perfect sense of right and wrong. In addition, we are not merely physical creatures; we are also spiritual creatures, which means we are somewhat like God, who is spirit. Our spirit is a reflection of God's nature and allows us to relate to him personally. To take another example, our ability to think about and process information is a reflection of God's knowledge. And our ability to relate to others, as well as our desire for community, is a reflection of God's perfect community within the Trinity. The Father, Son, and Holy Spirit have forever related to each other perfectly.

Because of sin, God's image in us is partly distorted. His image is not seen as clearly as it once was. Although the Bible is clear that man is still "made in the likeness of God" (James 3:9), that likeness, defiled by sin, doesn't look like everything it is supposed to. For example, sin distorts our moral judgment, clouds our thinking, and hinders our fellowship with others.

The good news is that God's image is being restored. God redeems his children through the life, death, and resurrection of Jesus so that they can be "conformed to the image of his Son" (Rom. 8:29), who is the "image of the invisible God" (Col. 1:15). Paul says that fellow Christians have a new nature, "which is being renewed in knowledge after the image of its creator" (Col. 3:10). And while here on earth, we "are being transformed" into Christ's image "from one degree of glory to another" (2 Cor. 3:18).

At the end of time, all of God's children will become like his Son, Jesus Christ. For, "just as we have borne the image of the man of dust, we shall also bear the image of the man of heaven" (1 Cor. 15:49). Christ "is the image of God" (2 Cor. 4:4) in a perfect sense. In Jesus we see God's likeness as it was intended to be. And because of Jesus, we will eventually be changed to reflect God's image as we were intended to do.

Responsibilities as Creatures
in God's Image

As creatures made in God's image, we were also made to be his representatives on the earth. Much like a king who places images of himself around his kingdom to show where he rules (images such as statues and pictures, for example), God has, through us, placed images of himself across his world. This is why he commanded Adam and Eve to "be fruitful and multiply and fill the earth" (Gen. 1:28). When they replicated God's image across the earth, they demonstrated all the places where God rules and reigns. And since "the earth is the LORD's and the fullness thereof" (Ps. 24:1), God desires that his image "fill the earth" (Gen. 1:28). When we fill the earth with God's image, we demonstrate all the places where he reigns and rules and bring him the glory he desires and deserves.

As God's representatives on the earth, we are also called to take care of his land. When God commanded Adam and Eve to "subdue" the earth and "have dominion over . . . every living thing that moves on the earth" (Gen. 1:28), he did so as a king telling his representatives to care for his kingdom in a way that honored him. Therefore, although we are free to take from the abundance of God's earth, we are to do so in a way that demonstrates care for it and respect for its Creator. And when we take the opportunity to make improvements to the world we live in, we are bringing God the glory he deserves by making his world look more like he designed it to look.

As God's image bearers—as representatives of the King of the universe—we have the awesome responsibility to help restore his people and his land to the way they were meant to be. We get the opportunity to work alongside the king who is "making all things new" (Rev. 21:5).

Therefore, we have great hope and respect for all people—regardless of their state. They, like us, are the culmination of God's infinitely wise and skillful creation. They have the potential to return to the beauty of Jesus Christ, the "image of the invisible God" (Col. 1:15), by turning away from their sin and turning to their Creator.

We also have great hope and respect for the world God has entrusted to us. We long to see it returned to its original state—a world without "thorns and thistles" (Gen. 3:18). And as we joyfully work toward this goal, we give God the glory we were created to bring to him.

Questions for Review and Application

1. Why were we created? What are some specific examples of ways we can fulfill the purpose for which we were created?
2. What does it mean to be created in God's image? How does that affect your view of yourself?
3. What are our responsibilities as God's image bearers? What are some ways you and your church can fulfill those responsibilities?

chapter

8

WHAT IS SIN?

S in disrupts everything. We don't live the lives we were originally designed to live, and we don't live in the world we were originally designed to live in. Sin mars the image of God in us; we no longer reflect the perfection God created us to reflect. Because of sin, things simply aren't the way they were originally meant to be. The story of the human race, as presented in the Bible, is the story of God fixing broken people living in a broken world. It is the story of God's victory over the many results of sin in the world.

What Sin Is

Sin is any failure to conform to the moral law of God in act, attitude, or nature. God sets forth his moral law in many places throughout the Bible. One such place is the Ten Commandments, found in Exodus 20:1–17. If sin is any action contrary to God's moral law, it makes sense that Exodus 20:13 says, "You shall not murder," and Exodus 20:15 says, "You shall not steal." But sin is also found in attitudes contrary to God's moral law. This is why Exodus 20:17 says, "You shall not covet your neighbor's house; you shall not covet your neighbor's wife." Sin is also found in our nature—the internal character that is the essence of who we are. This is why Paul says that those who reject Jesus are "by nature children of wrath" (Eph. 2:3).

God is eternally good in his character; all that he is conforms perfectly to his moral law. Therefore, anything contrary to his moral law is contrary to his character, that is, contrary to God himself. God hates sin because it directly contradicts everything he is.

Where Sin Came From

Since sin is in complete contradiction to God, he cannot sin, and we should never blame God for sin or think that he bears the responsibility for sin. God's "work is perfect" and "all his ways are justice. A God of faithfulness and without iniquity, just and upright is he" (Deut. 32:4). It is impossible for God even to desire to do wrong, "for God cannot be tempted with evil, and he himself tempts no one" (James 1:13). Yet the Bible also says that God "works all things according to the counsel of his will" (Eph. 1:11), so it seems that God somehow ordained that sin would come into the world. Sin did not surprise God when it came into the world, nor did it overpower him. Instead, God decided that he would allow moral creatures to willfully and voluntarily choose to sin. How we put these two truths together is one of the most difficult questions in theology, and it is healthy for us to allow a substantial element of mystery, admitting that a full understanding is beyond anyone's ability in this age. (The recognition that there is mystery here should also guard us against getting into heated arguments over this topic!)

Sin existed in Satan and his demons before the disobedience of Adam and Eve, and then it entered the world of humans through their decisions. God told Adam, "of the tree of the knowledge of good and evil you shall not eat" (Gen. 2:17). So when Adam and Eve ate from the tree (Gen. 3:6), they directly contradicted God's command. Neither God nor Satan forced them to eat from the tree; they did so willingly and thus willingly sinned against God.

As a result, Adam's nature became sinful. Sin became something Adam naturally did. Adam's sin also caused us to inherit a sinful nature, one that is naturally opposed to God and his moral law. That is why Paul said, "I know that nothing good dwells in me" (Rom. 7:18). It is why Jeremiah said, "The heart is deceitful above all things, and desperately sick; who can understand it?" (Jer. 17:9). It is why David said, "I was brought forth in iniquity, and in sin did my mother conceive me" (Ps. 51:5). It is why "the wicked . . . go astray from birth" (Ps. 58:3).

Although our inherited tendency to sin does not mean we are as bad as we could be, it does mean that we, like Adam after he sinned, are unable on our own to do anything that pleases God. We lack any spiritual good in ourselves, and therefore we are unable to do any spiritual good before God. Although from a human standpoint we may be able to do things that seem to be good, to God "all our righteous deeds are like a polluted garment" (Isa. 64:6).

Every part of our being is affected by sin—our intellects, our emotions, our desires, our hearts, our goals, our motives, and even our physical bodies. All are subject to the decay and destruction caused by sin. Our actions, our attitudes, and our very natures all make us guilty of sin.

We received not only Adam's sinful nature, but also his sin-produced guilt. Adam's action resulted not only in his own guilt, but also in the guilt of every other human. As Paul explains, "Sin came into the world through one man, and death through sin, and so death spread to all men because all sinned" (Rom. 5:12). And "by the one man's disobedience the many were made sinners" (Rom. 5:19). Therefore, when Adam sinned, God thought of us all as having sinned.

Although this may seem unfair and difficult to actually believe, it is very consistent with the pattern of God. "For as by the one man's disobedience the many were made sinners, so by the one man's obedience the many will be made righteous" (Rom. 5:19). God considers the human race as organically whole—a unity, represented by Adam as its head. He also, as is clear from Romans 5:19, considers a new race of Christians as organically whole—a unity, represented by Christ as its head. We cannot accept the second statement without accepting the first.

Even if we don't believe we are considered guilty because of Adam's sin, we all would admit we have contradicted God's moral law either in attitude or action. And so we all are guilty of sin and in need of a way to make ourselves right with God. The good news is that God has designed the world in such a way that our individual failings can be redeemed through the work of another. Our individual disobedience can be made right by the obedience of another. Our individual sin can be removed by the sinlessness of another. As we read in Romans 5:18–19, "Therefore, as one trespass led to condemnation for all men, so one act of righteousness leads to justification and life for all men. For as by the one man's disobedience the many were made sinners, so by the one man's obedience the many will be made righteous."

How Sin Affects Us

Scripture is clear: "There is no one who does not sin" (1 Kings 8:46); "There is none who does good, not even one"

(Ps. 14:3); "All have sinned and fall short of the glory of God" (Rom. 3:23); and as John tells us, "If we say we have no sin, we deceive ourselves, and the truth is not in us" (1 John 1:8). Therefore, all stand guilty before God.

God said the penalty for eating of the Tree of the Knowledge of Good and Evil was death (Gen. 2:17). Death, Paul tells us, is actually the penalty for all sin: "The wages of sin is death" (Rom. 6:23). But just as God didn't bring the penalty of death immediately on Adam and Eve, so he doesn't bring the penalty of death immediately upon us. In fact, through Jesus' life, death, and resurrection, God offers us freedom from the condemnation sin brings. Peter says about Jesus, "He himself bore our sins in his body on the tree, that we might die to sin and live to righteousness" (1 Peter 2:24). For those who look to Jesus for the forgiveness of their sins, "there is therefore now no condemnation" (Rom. 8:1).

So, when we sin as forgiven Christians, our legal standing before God is not affected. We are still forgiven because Christ's death paid for all of our sins. As Paul tells us, "Christ died for our sins" (1 Cor. 15:3)—without any distinction among past, present, and future sins. Although John tells us we all sin, he also affirms that even in our sin "we are God's children now" (1 John 3:2).

While sin does not affect our status or standing with God, it does affect our fellowship with God, for God is grieved by our sin. This can often result in God's discipline in our lives since "the Lord disciplines the one he loves" (Heb. 12:6). This loving discipline is "for our good, that we may share his holiness" (Heb. 12:10). Sin can also affect our relationships with others. Sinful words or actions can result in a broken relationship, even between Christians.

Even though all Christians still sin, they should not

participate in a long-term pattern of greater and greater dis-obedience to God's moral law, for "no one born of God makes a practice of sinning" (1 John 3:9). But if a person makes a practice of sinning, that is, if someone continues in a pattern of disobedience without repentance, he may not have ever truly put his trust in Jesus for salvation. That is, the sinful pattern of his life could show that he never really was a Christian.

In contrast, when Christians sin, they should earnestly and quickly "confess" their sins to God. When we do so, we will find God is "faithful and just to forgive us our sins and to cleanse us from all unrighteousness" (1 John 1:9).

Questions for Review and Application

1. What is sin? How does it affect our lives and the world we live in?
2. Will Christians continue to sin? Why or why not?
3. What are some of the negative results of sin in the life of a Christian? What should Christians do if they sin?
4. How was sin defeated? How does this make you feel? Take a moment to pray, telling God how his defeat of sin makes you feel.

chapter 9

WHO IS CHRIST?

In the person of Jesus, God physically entered into our world. An infinite God came to live in a finite world. The One who knew exactly how things were supposed to be came to a place where things obviously weren't how they were supposed to be. In Jesus, God and man became one person, a person unlike anyone else the world has ever seen or will ever see. Jesus Christ was, and forever will be, fully God and fully man in one person. And that one person changed the course of history forever.

Jesus—Fully Man

Jesus was fully and completely human. He was conceived in the womb of his mother by a miraculous work of the Holy Spirit. This is made clear in Matthew 1:18: "Now the birth of Jesus Christ took place in this way. When his mother Mary had been betrothed to Joseph, before they came together she was found to be with child from the Holy Spirit." While many things could be said about this, one thing is clear: Jesus was born of a human mother. His ordinary human birth affirms his humanity.

Just as we have a human body, so did Jesus. As a child, he

"grew and became strong" (Luke 2:40), and as he grew older, he "increased in wisdom and in stature and in favor with God and man" (Luke 2:52). He became "wearied" from a journey (John 4:6); after a fast, "he was hungry" (Matt. 4:2); and while on the cross, he said, "I thirst" (John 19:28). His body was, in every respect, just like ours.

Jesus rose from the dead in a physical, human body that was no longer subject to weakness, disease, or death. As he told his disciples, who were astonished at the risen Christ, "See my hands and my feet, that it is I myself. Touch me, and see. For a spirit does not have flesh and bones as you see that I have" (Luke 24:39). Jesus continues to reside in this perfect but human body in heaven.

Jesus' mind was like ours as well. He went through a learning process as other children do. Luke, for example, tells us Jesus "increased in wisdom" (Luke 2:52). Like a normal child, he learned how to do things such as talk, read, write, and eat. In his human nature he did not know the day when he would return to earth: "But concerning that day or that hour, no one knows, not even the angels in heaven, nor the Son, but only the Father" (Mark 13:32).

In addition, Jesus felt the full range of emotions: he "marveled" at the faith of the centurion (Matt. 8:10); he "wept" at the death of his friend Lazarus (John 11:35); and he prayed to God "with loud cries and tears" (Heb. 5:7). Before his crucifixion he said, "My soul is very sorrowful, even to death" (Matt. 26:38) and "Now is my soul troubled" (John 12:27).

Jesus was like us in every respect but one: he was without sin. That is why at the end of his life he could say, "I have kept my Father's commandments and abide in his love" (John 15:10). And that is why Paul referred to Jesus as "him . . . who knew no sin" (2 Cor. 5:21). Peter tells us that Jesus "committed no sin, neither was deceit found in his mouth" (1 Peter 2:22). John tells us that "in him there is no sin" (1 John 3:5). Clearly, Jesus is "one who in every respect has been tempted as we are, yet without sin" (Heb. 4:15).

Jesus had to be fully human to serve as our perfectly obedient representative. His representative obedience as a man is in contrast to Adam's representative disobedience. Paul says that "as by the one man's disobedience the many were made sinners, so by the one man's obedience the many will be made righteous" (Rom. 5:19). If Jesus wasn't fully human, his obedience in our place would be meaningless.

Just as Jesus had to be human to live in our place, he also had to be human to die in our place. This was necessary because of our humanity. As Hebrews 2:17 tells us, "He had to be made like his brothers in every respect, so that he might become a merciful and faithful high priest in the service of God, to make propitiation for the sins of the people." If Jesus weren't fully human, his death in our place would be meaningless.

In addition, Jesus' humanity (as well as his deity) allows him to serve as the "one mediator between God and men" (1 Tim. 2:5). It also means that as a man, he was "in every respect . . . tempted as we are" and so is able to "sympathize with our weaknesses" (Heb. 4:15). "Because he himself has suffered when tempted, he is able to help those who are being tempted" (Heb. 2:18).

Jesus—Fully God

As I stated earlier, Jesus was conceived in the womb of his mother by a miraculous work of the Holy Spirit. Again, this is made clear in Matthew 1:18. Jesus' virgin birth was a supernatural work of God. Through the work of the Holy Spirit inside Jesus' mother, Mary, the human and the divine were united in a way they never will be in any other person.

As we saw when we discussed the full deity of the Trinity (see chapter 3), the Bible clearly says that Jesus is fully God. For example, Paul writes of Jesus in Colossians 2:9, "In him the whole fullness of deity dwells bodily." In addition, when Jesus' contemporaries called him "Lord," they were employing a term that was used over six thousand times in the Greek translation of the Old Testament to refer to God or "the Lord." Therefore, when the angels announced Jesus' birth by saying, "For unto you is born this day in the city of David a Savior, who is Christ the Lord" (Luke 2:11), they were saying that the Lord God himself was born.

When asked if he had seen Abraham, Jesus responded by saying, "Before Abraham was, I am" (John 8:57–58). Those who heard him say this "picked up stones to throw at him" (John 8:59), which is what any self-respecting religious leader would have done if someone claimed to be God. They understood that Jesus was claiming the same title God claimed for himself in Exodus 3:14—"I AM WHO I AM."

In Revelation 22:13 Jesus says, "I am the Alpha and the Omega, the first and the last, the beginning and the end." This is very similar to what God the Father said at the beginning of the same book: "'I am the Alpha and the Omega,' says the Lord God, 'who is and who was and who is to come, the Almighty'" (Rev. 1:8).

The prophet Isaiah affirms Jesus as the King who reigns forever—a role only God could fill: "Of the increase of his government and of peace there will be no end" (Isa. 9:7). That is why Paul said that Jesus is worthy of worship: "God has highly exalted him and bestowed on him the name that is above every name, so that at the name of Jesus every knee should bow, in heaven and on earth and under the earth, and every tongue confess that Jesus Christ is Lord, to the glory of God the Father" (Phil. 2:9–11). Jesus' divinity is the reason God the Father says, "Let all God's angels worship him" (Heb. 1:6).

Jesus was fully God. "In him all the fullness of God was pleased to dwell" (Col. 1:19). If Jesus wasn't fully God, he could not have borne the full penalty for sin for the whole world. And if he didn't bear the full penalty of sin for the world as a sinless man, there would be no valid payment for anyone's sins, and nobody could be saved.

Jesus—Fully God and Fully Man in One Person

Jesus was fully God. Jesus was also fully man. He was fully both at the same time. The eternal Son of God took to himself a truly human nature. His divine and human natures are forever distinct and retain their own properties even though they are eternally and inseparably united together in one person.

This is probably the most amazing miracle of the entire Bible—the eternal Son of God, himself fully God, became fully man and in doing so joined himself to a human nature forever. Jesus, a man unlike anyone else the world will ever see again, by eternally bringing together both the infinite and the finite, changed the course of history forever.

Questions for Review and Application

1. Jesus is fully God. What are some ways that this encourages you?
2. Jesus is fully man. What are some ways that this encourages you?
3. Take a moment to pray and talk directly to Jesus, thanking him for coming to earth and becoming fully man for your sake.

WHAT IS THE ATONEMENT?

Prior to Jesus' birth, an angel told his earthly father, Joseph, that he was to name the baby in Mary's womb Jesus, "for he will save his people from their sins" (Matt. 1:21). Jesus did save his people from their sins—both through the life he lived and through the death he died. The work Jesus did in living and dying to earn our salvation is sometimes referred to as the atonement.

The Cause of the Atonement

Scripture is clear: Christ came to earn our salvation because of God's faithful love (or mercy) and justice. God's love is affirmed in John 3:16: "For God so loved the world, that he gave his only Son, that whoever believes in him should not perish but have eternal life." God's justice is affirmed when Paul writes that God put forward Jesus "as a propitiation" (Rom. 3:25), that is, a sacrifice that bears God's wrath so that God looks favorably toward us. Paul says this was done "to show God's righteousness" and also "so that he might be just" (Rom. 3:25–26). In other words, the sins God "passed over" or didn't punish before Christ came to earth had to be punished somehow if God was to "be just." Therefore, someone had to take the punishment for those sins, and that someone was Jesus. In Jesus' life and death, we find a full expression of God's justice (sin is punished) and faithful love (God gave his own Son to bear the punishment).

The Necessity of the Atonement

Although it was not necessary that God save any people at all, in his love he chose to save some. Once he made that decision, God's justice made it necessary for Christ to live the life he lived and die the death he died.

After Jesus rose from the dead, he rhetorically asked, "Was it not necessary that the Christ should suffer these things and enter into his glory?" (Luke 24:26). Jesus knew there was no other way for God to save us than for him to die in our place. Jesus had to suffer and die for our sins. Other means, like the sacrifices offered for sins in the Old Testament, had no lasting value, for "it is impossible for the blood of bulls and goats to take away sins" (Heb. 10:4). Jesus, "by means of his own blood," secured "an eternal redemption" (Heb. 9:12), thereby putting away sin "by the sacrifice of himself" (Heb. 9:26).

The Nature of the Atonement

And yet if Christ had only offered himself as a sacrifice, thereby earning us forgiveness of sins, we would only have access to a partial salvation. Although our guilt would be removed, we would be like Adam and Eve when they were first created: guilt-free but capable of sin and having no lifelong record of obedience. And in order to enter into fellowship with God, we would need to live a life of perfect obedience.

Therefore, Christ had to live a life of perfect obedience to God so that the positive merits of that obedience could be counted for us. This is what Paul means when he says, "By the one man's obedience the many will be made righteous" (Rom. 5:19). And this is why Paul does not count on his own righteousness, but instead counts on "that which comes through faith in Christ, the righteousness from God that depends on faith" (Phil. 3:9). Christ, through the sinless life he lived, became our righteousness (1 Cor. 1:30).

Jesus also lived a life of suffering. He was, in the words of Isaiah, "despised and rejected by men, a man of sorrows and acquainted with grief" (Isa. 53:3). He suffered when he was assaulted by Satan's attacks and temptations in the wilderness (Matt. 4:1–11). He "endured from sinners" tremendous "hostility against himself" (Heb. 12:3). He was tremendously grieved at the death of his close friend Lazarus (John 11:35). It was through these and other sufferings that "he learned obedience" (though he never once disobeyed) and "became the source of eternal salvation to all who obey him" (Heb. 5:8–9).

As Jesus drew closer to his death, his sufferings increased. He told his disciples something of the agony he was experiencing when he said, "My soul is very sorrowful, even to death" (Matt. 26:38). When Jesus was crucified, he suffered one of the most horrible forms of death ever devised by man. While he did not necessarily suffer more pain than any human being has ever suffered, the pain he experienced was immense.

When crucified, Christ was forced to endure a slow death by suffocation, brought on by the weight of his own body. He was stretched out and fastened by nails to the cross. His arms supported most of the weight of his body. His chest cavity was pulled upward and outward, making it difficult to exhale and then draw in a fresh breath. To breathe, he had to push up with his legs, putting all the weight on the nails through his feet, and pull up on the nails through his hands, sending fiery pain through the nerves of his arms and legs. His back, already whipped raw, scraped against the rough, splinter-filled wooden cross with each breath he took.

But the physical pain was nothing compared to the spiritual pain. Jesus never sinned. Jesus hated sin. Yet Jesus voluntarily took upon himself all the sins of those who one day would be saved. "He bore the sin of many" (Isa. 53:12). That which he hated with his whole being was poured out on him. As Peter tells us, "He himself bore our sins in his body on the tree, that we might die to sin and live to righteousness. By his wounds you have been healed" (1 Peter 2:24). "For our sake," God made Christ "to be sin" (2 Cor. 5:21). Jesus became "a curse for us" to redeem us "from the curse of the law" (Gal. 3:13).

And Jesus faced this all alone. "All the disciples left him and fled" (Matt. 26:56). God, his Father, abandoned him. Jesus cried, "My God, my God, why have you forsaken me?" (Matt. 27:46), because at that time he was cut off from the sweet fellowship with his heavenly Father that had been the unfailing source of inward strength and the element of greatest joy in a life filled with sorrow. And at the height of his suffering, he was very much alone.

Even more difficult than the physical pain, mental anguish, and complete abandonment was the pain of bearing the full wrath of God upon himself. As Jesus bore the guilt of our sins, God unleashed all wrath and punishment for our sins upon his own Son. Jesus became the object of the intense hatred of sin and vengeance against sin that God had patiently stored up since the beginning of the world.

Again, Jesus said of himself that it was "necessary that the Christ should suffer these things" (Luke 24:26). This includes being made a "propitiation" (Rom. 3:25), a sacrifice that bears God's full wrath toward sin. God made "him [Jesus] to be sin who knew no sin" (2 Cor. 5:21). God thought of Christ as sin and therefore treated him as sin. There was no other way. God's justice required it. This act of divine justice was also an act of divine love for us. "For our sake he made him to be sin who knew no sin, so that in him we might become the righteousness of God" (2 Cor. 5:21).

Christ necessarily and willingly bore the full punishment for our sin on the cross. And so through his death, God's justice was met. Christ "put away sin by the sacrifice of himself" (Heb. 9:26).

The Result of the Atonement

Christ lived a perfect, sinless life and died a horrific, sinner's death in order to "save his people from their sins" (Matt. 1:21). He paid the penalty we deserved to pay for our sin. He bore the wrath we deserved to bear. He overcame the separation our sin caused between God and us. He freed us from the bondage caused by sin. Because of Christ's work on our behalf, God "delivered us from the domain of darkness" and transferred "us to the kingdom of his beloved Son" (Col. 1:13). What a great salvation!

Questions for Review and Application

1. Why was it necessary for Jesus to come and live a perfect life on earth?

2. Why was it necessary that Jesus die? Could he have saved us in some other way?

3. How does your understanding of the atonement humble you? How does it encourage you?

chapter 11

WHAT IS THE RESURRECTION?

Jesus' work on earth didn't end with his life and death. If it had ended there, "our preaching is in vain . . . your faith is in vain . . . your faith is futile," and "we are of all people most to be pitied" (1 Cor. 15:14–19). But Jesus rose from the dead and ascended into heaven a victorious, conquering King.

Details of the Resurrection

All four gospels contain accounts of Jesus' resurrection (Matt. 28:1–20; Mark 16:1–8; Luke 24:1–53; John 20:1–21:25). Throughout the book of Acts, the apostles continually speak of Jesus' resurrection, encouraging people to trust in him as the One who is alive and reigning in heaven. The rest of the New Testament depends entirely on the assumption that Jesus is a living, reigning Savior who is the head of the newly formed church. Simply put, one can find ample proof for the resurrection throughout the New Testament.

Christ's resurrection was not a simple coming back from the dead as others had experienced (such as Lazarus in John 11:1–44). Rather, when Jesus rose from the dead, he began a new kind of human life in which he had a perfect body that was no longer subject to weakness, aging, death, or decay. When Jesus rose from the dead, he had a body that would live eternally, for Jesus had "put on the imperishable"; he had "put on immortality" (1 Cor. 15:53).

Jesus' new body was a physical body. When his disciples saw him, they "took hold of his feet" (Matt. 28:9). His disciples "ate and drank with him after he rose from the dead" (Acts 10:41). In his new body, Jesus "took . . . bread and blessed and broke it" (Luke 24:30). He also invited Thomas to touch his hands and side (John 20:27). The Bible is clear: Jesus physically rose from the dead with a body made of "flesh and bones" (Luke 24:39).

Results of the Resurrection

Consequently, all who look to Jesus for their salvation have been "born again to a living hope through the resurrection of Jesus Christ from the dead" (1 Peter 1:3). That is, Christ earned for us a new future life that is like his own. Although our bodies are not yet like his new body, our spirits have already been made alive with new resurrection power.

This resurrection power helps us live the lives we were made to live. It gives us the power to gain more and more victory over sin in our lives. Because of the resurrection, we can consider ourselves "dead to sin" (Rom. 6:11). Although we will not attain sinless perfection in this life, Paul still tells us that "sin will have no dominion" over us (Rom. 6:14); it will not rule us or control us. This resurrection power also includes power from the Holy Spirit, which enables us to do the work Jesus commissioned us to do (Acts 1:8).

In addition, Jesus' resurrection insures our right standing

before God. Paul, in Romans 4:25, says Jesus was "raised for our justification." When God raised Jesus from the dead, he was affirming Jesus' work on our behalf. He was demonstrating his approval of Jesus' work of suffering and dying for our sins. He was affirming that Jesus' work on our behalf was complete; the penalty for sin was paid, and therefore Jesus did not need to remain dead any longer. As Hebrews 1:3 tells us, "After making purification for sins, he sat down at the right hand of the Majesty on high." Jesus sat down at God's right hand because his work was complete.

Finally, since "God raised the Lord," he "will also raise us up by his power" (1 Cor. 6:14). And "he who raised the Lord Jesus will raise us also with Jesus and bring us . . . into his presence" (2 Cor. 4:14). Jesus' resurrection means we will also experience a resurrection of our own. Paul says that in Jesus' resurrection we see a picture of what is to come for us (1 Cor. 15:20). When Jesus returns, "we shall all be changed" (1 Cor. 15:51); our mortal body will be exchanged for an immortal one (1 Cor. 15:53). At the final resurrection, our resurrection, we will receive a new body just like the one Jesus now inhabits.

Jesus' Ascension

Forty days after his resurrection (Acts 1:3), Jesus led his followers just outside Jerusalem "and lifting up his hands he blessed them. While he blessed them, he parted from them and was carried up into heaven" (Luke 24:50–51). When Jesus left the earth, he left for a specific place: heaven.

Once in heaven, Jesus was "exalted at the right hand of God" (Acts 2:33). God "highly exalted him and bestowed on him the name that is above every name" (Phil. 2:9). After his ascension, Jesus received glory, honor, and authority that had never been his before as one who was both God and man. Angelic choirs now sing praise to him with the words, "Worthy is the Lamb who was slain, to receive power and wealth and wisdom and might and honor and glory and blessing!" (Rev. 5:12). Now at God's right hand, Christ "must reign until he has put all his enemies under his feet" (1 Cor. 15:25).

Christ's life provides a pattern for ours. Just as his resurrection lets us know what will eventually happen to us, his ascension lets us know where we will eventually go. And so we wait "with eager longing" (Rom. 8:19) for Christ's return when we will be taken from this world into a glorious new one. Then we, with our new perfect bodies, will live forever in our new perfect world.

Questions for Review and Application

1. Why is it important that Jesus rose from the dead? What would your life be like if he had not risen from the dead?
2. What are some results in your life, and in the whole world, of Jesus' resurrection from the dead?
3. What about Jesus' resurrection makes you long for your own resurrection?

12

WHAT IS ELECTION?

There has been much controversy inside and outside of the church regarding the doctrine of election (sometimes also called "predestination"). We may define election as follows: Election is an act of God before creation in which he chooses some people to be saved, not on account of any foreseen merit in them, but only because of his sovereign good pleasure. Many have thought that this doctrine, defined in this way, is troubling and unfair. Before jumping to conclusions, however, it is important to see where this definition, and therefore this doctrine, comes from.

New Testament Teachings on Election

Several passages in the New Testament seem to affirm quite clearly that God ordained beforehand those who would be saved. For example, when Paul and Barnabas began to preach to the Gentiles in Antioch in Pisidia, Luke writes, "And when the Gentiles heard this, they began rejoicing and glorifying the word of the Lord, and as many as were appointed to eternal life believed" (Acts 13:48).

One of the reasons Luke says, almost in passing, that many were "appointed to eternal life" is that he understood the truth

Paul would later express in Ephesians 1:4–6: God "chose us in him [Christ] before the foundation of the world, that we should be holy and blameless before him. In love he predestined us for adoption to himself as sons through Jesus Christ, according to the purpose of his will, to the praise of his glorious grace." Paul later adds that "we who were the first to hope in Christ" are to live for "the praise of his glory" (Eph. 1:12).

God saved us and called us to himself, not because of our goodness, but because of his own purpose and his unmerited grace in eternity past. Paul says that God is the One "who saved us and called us to a holy calling, not because of our works but because of his own purpose and grace, which he gave us in Christ Jesus before the ages began" (2 Tim. 1:9).

John's vision in Revelation tells us that individual salvation—in this passage spoken of as those whose names are written in the book of life—was determined "from the foundation of the world" (Rev. 17:8).

What This Means

It is important to note that these New Testament authors often present the doctrine of election as a comfort to all who believe in Jesus. For example, Paul says that God has acted and always will act for the good of those whom he called to himself: "And we know that for those who love God all things work together for good, for those who are called according to his purpose" (Rom. 8:28).

But how could Paul know this? He gives the reason in the next two verses. He can say this because when he looks into the distant past, before the creation of the world, he sees that God "foreknew" and "predestined" his people "to be conformed to the image of his Son" (Rom. 8:29). Then, when Paul looks at the recent past, he finds that "those whom he [God] predestined he also called, and those whom he called he also justified" (Rom. 8:30). And when Paul looks toward the future, he sees that "those whom he [God] justified he also glorified" (Rom. 8:30), in the sense that God has already determined he will someday give perfect, glorified bodies to those who believe in Christ. From eternity to eternity God has acted and will act with the good of his people in mind. Election is thus a cause for comfort and for assurance that God will work for our good today. And this will all happen "not because of our works but because of his own purpose and grace, which he gave us in Christ Jesus before the ages began" (2 Tim. 1:9).

A natural response to God's work on our behalf is that we would live "to the praise of his glory" (Eph. 1:12). We can, as Paul did, give thanks to God for those he has chosen (1 Thess. 1:2–4), knowing that God is the one ultimately responsible for their salvation and all the good things that accompany it. In fact, Paul says we are obligated to give thanks to God for such a great salvation (1 Thess. 2:13). Singing praises to God for salvation does not leave any room for singing our own praises, because our salvation is not our own work but is a gift from God (Eph. 2:8–9).

Yet this truth should not lead us to think that our work of evangelism is unimportant! When God chooses people to be saved, he carries this out through human means. That is why Paul worked so hard at preaching the gospel. He said, "I endure everything for the sake of the elect, that they also may obtain the salvation that is in Christ Jesus with eternal glory" (2 Tim. 2:10). Paul knew that God has chosen some people to be saved, and he saw this as an encouragement— not discouragement—to preach the gospel, even if it meant enduring great suffering. Election was Paul's guarantee that there would be some success for his evangelism, for he knew that *some* of the people he spoke to would be the elect and that they would believe the gospel and be saved. It is as if someone invited Paul to come fishing and said, "I guarantee that you will catch some fish—they are hungry and waiting."

What This Doesn't Mean

Affirming the doctrine of election does *not* mean that our choices don't matter and our actions don't have any consequences. Nor does the doctrine of election require us to affirm an impersonal, inflexible universe that is controlled by an impersonal, inflexible force.

The New Testament presents the entire outworking of salvation as something brought about by a personal God deeply in love with personal creatures. "In love he predestined us for adoption to himself as sons through Jesus Christ" (Eph. 1:4–5). God's act of election was permeated with personal love for those whom he chose (see also John 3:16; Rom. 8:28).

Moreover, Scripture continually views us as *personal* creatures who make *willing choices* to accept or reject the gospel. For example, this is seen clearly in the invitation at the end of Revelation: "The Spirit and the Bride say, 'Come.' And let the one who hears say, 'Come.' And let the one who is thirsty come; let the one who desires take the water of life without price" (22:17). This invitation and many others like it (for example, Matt. 11:28) are addressed to genuine persons who are capable of hearing the invitation and responding to it by a decision of their wills. These real decisions have eternal consequences, as is shown in John 3:18: "Whoever believes in him is not condemned, but whoever does not believe is condemned already, because he has not believed in the name of the only Son of God."

While a proper understanding of election does give real value to our decisions and choices, it does not mean that God's decision was *based on* our choices. When God chose individuals "before the foundation of the world" (Eph. 1:4), he did not do so because he foresaw their faith or some decision they would make. Paul affirms this in Romans 8:29 when he writes, "For those whom he foreknew he also predestined." When Paul speaks about God's foreknowledge, he is thinking of God as knowing *persons* ("those whom"). God "foreknew" these individuals in the context of a saving relationship with them. This is different from speaking about foreknowledge of an individual's actions or decisions, such as a decision to believe.

In fact, Scripture never speaks of faith (present or future) as the reason God chose someone. In Ephesians 1:4–6 Paul says, "In love he predestined us for adoption to himself as sons through Jesus Christ, *according to the purpose of his will*, to the praise of his glorious grace." If election were ultimately based on our decision, it would seem to diminish God's love, cheapen his grace (for there would be some merit on our part), and diminish the glory that is due him for our salvation.

Are We Really Free?

Many believe that if the doctrine of election is true, then we aren't really free. The difficulty in thinking this way is that many different definitions and assumptions surround the word *free*, and these differences easily lead to misunderstanding and disagreement. In this case it is helpful to use a term other than *free* so as to communicate more carefully what we want to say. For example, the Bible appeals to our ability to make *voluntary* choices or *willing* choices hundreds of times (see the verses above concerning our "willing choice" and also all the commands in the Bible that ask us to respond and obey). We aren't forced to make choices contrary to our own will. We ultimately do what we *desire* to do. Making choices is part of what it means to be a human being in God's image, for we imitate God's own activity of deciding to do things that are consistent with his character.

But does that mean that God had nothing to do with our choices? Do we want to insist that God, our infinitely powerful and wise Creator, cannot influence and mold and shape our hearts and our desires according to his plan? In fact, if God works *through* our choices and desires to bring about his plan, this preserves our ability to choose willingly while at the same time assuring that our choices will be in accord with what God decided and ordained would happen.

Therefore, if we respond to Christ's invitation in a positive way, we can honestly say that we *chose* to respond to Christ while also saying that it was (in ways we cannot fully understand) ordained by God. If we can't fully understand how these two things can be true at the same time, then we must acknowledge that there is mystery here. At least in this age, we cannot completely grasp this mystery. And although we do not understand it, we should at least be sure that we speak the way the Bible speaks about this in all aspects of its teaching.

Furthermore, God also created us so that our choices would be *real choices*. However, our choices do not need to be absolutely free of any involvement by God in order to be real, voluntary, willing choices. To take another example, while we make the choice to breathe many times every day, God, as our Creator and Sustainer, is intricately involved with us in that decision, for God "works all things according to the counsel of his will" (Eph. 1:11), and Christ continually "upholds the universe by the word of his power" (Heb. 1:3).

What about those who do not believe, those whom God has not "elected" or chosen? The Bible never puts any blame on God for anyone's rejection of Christ's claims. The emphasis is always on the willing choices of those who refuse to believe, and the blame for their unbelief rests with them. As Jesus said in John 8:43–44, "Why do you not understand what I say? It is because you cannot bear to hear my word. You are of your father the devil, and your will is to do your father's desires." To some who rejected him earlier, Jesus said, "You refuse to come to me that you may have life" (John 5:40). And Paul, in Romans 1:20, says that all who reject the clear revelation of God given to all mankind are "without excuse." This is the consistent pattern in Scripture: People who remain in unbelief do so because they are unwilling to come to God, and the blame for such unbelief always lies with the unbelievers themselves, never with God. Once again, we probably will not be able to fully understand in this age just how this can be so.

Is God Really Fair?

At this point some people will object that if the doctrine of election is true, then God isn't really fair. Since God chooses some to be saved and passes over others, deciding not to save them, his grace is awarded rather unfairly.

It is important to understand what "fair" really is with respect to salvation. Indeed, it would be perfectly fair for God not to save *any* human beings who sinned and rebelled against him, just as he did with the angels: "God did not spare angels when they sinned, but cast them into hell and committed them to chains of gloomy darkness to be kept until the judgment"

(2 Peter 2:4). But if he does save any human beings, then this is a demonstration of grace, which goes far beyond the requirements of fairness and justice. If God saved only five people out of the whole human race, this would be mercy and grace. If he saved one hundred, this would be amazing mercy and grace. But in fact he has decided to save "a great multitude that no one could number, from every nation, from all tribes and peoples and languages" (Rev. 7:9). This is mercy and grace beyond our comprehension.

Paul raises this question on a deeper level in Romans 9. After saying that God "has mercy on whomever he wills, and he hardens whomever he wills" (v. 18), Paul then writes, "You will say to me then, 'Why does he still find fault? For who can resist his will?'" (v. 19). In essence, Paul is giving voice to a very common question: If each person's ultimate destiny is determined by God, then how can this be fair? Even when people make willing choices, determining whether they will be saved or not, if God is actually somehow behind those choices, then how can he be fair?

Here is what Paul says:

> But who are you, O man, to answer back to God? Will what is molded say to its molder, "Why have you made me like this?" Has the potter no right over the clay, to make out of the same lump one vessel for honorable use and another for dishonorable use? What if God, desiring to show his wrath and to make known his power, has endured with much patience vessels of wrath prepared for destruction, in order to make known the riches of his glory for vessels of mercy, which he has prepared beforehand for glory—even us whom he has called, not from the Jews only but also from the Gentiles? (Romans 9:20–24)

Paul is essentially saying that there is a point beyond which we cannot answer back to God or question his justice. God has done what he has done according to his sovereign will. He is the Creator; we are the creatures, and we ultimately have no basis from which to accuse him of unfairness or injustice. Our response to these words in Romans reveals a lot about our hearts and our willingness to submit to our sovereign Creator.

Does God Want Everyone to Be Saved?

If election is true, then does God still want everybody to be saved? Yes, according to some Scripture passages. In 1 Timothy 2:4 Paul writes of our God and Savior "who desires all people to be saved and to come to the knowledge of the truth." Peter says the same thing in 2 Peter 3:9 when he writes that the Lord "is patient toward you, not wishing that any should perish, but that all should reach repentance."

While people will disagree on the interpretation of these verses, most will agree, on reflection, that there are some things that God desires more than others. Oftentimes people who do not agree with the doctrine of election will say, based on these verses and others, that God desires to preserve man's free will more than he desires to save every person. But people who support the doctrine of election will say that God desires to further his glory more than he desires to save every person, and that passages like Romans 9 indicate that his glory is furthered by saving some people but not all. (Christians on both sides of the debate agree that not everybody will be saved.)

How then can both sides say that God *desires* everyone to be saved, in accordance with verses like 1 Timothy 2:4 and 2 Peter 3:9? These verses tell us what God commands people to do and what actions please him (namely, repenting and believing in Christ). In this sense he truly "desires" and "wishes" that every person be saved. This is what is sometimes called his "revealed" will, what he tells everybody on earth they should do. But such verses are not talking about God's secret, hidden plans from all eternity to choose some people to be saved.

The fact that not everyone will be saved is one of the most difficult doctrines in Scripture to consider. The Bible indicates that even God has great sorrow when he thinks about those who will not be saved. "As I live, declares the Lord GOD, I have no pleasure in the death of the wicked, but that the wicked turn from his way and live; turn back, turn back from your evil ways, for why will you die, O house of Israel?" (Ezek. 33:11). When Jesus thought of the people who rejected him in Jerusalem, "he wept over it" (Luke 19:41), and he said, "O Jerusalem, Jerusalem, the city that kills the prophets and stones those who are sent to it! How often would I have gathered your children together as a hen gathers her brood under her wings, and you were not willing!" (Matt. 23:37). And the apostle Paul says, "I have great sorrow and unceasing anguish in my heart" (Rom. 9:2) when he thinks about his Jewish brothers and sisters who have rejected Christ. The love God gives us for our fellow human beings and the love he commands us to have for our neighbors causes us great sorrow when we realize that not everyone will be saved. And yet the punishment of sinners is a righteous outworking of God's justice, and we should not think that it is wrong.

In addition, God gives all human beings innumerable blessings in this life that are not part of salvation. This doctrine is sometimes called "common grace" because it refers to a manifestation of God's grace that is common to all people and is different from God's saving grace.

Common Grace

When any of us sin, we deserve one thing: eternal separation from God. We deserve to be cut off from experiencing any good from God and to live forever in hell, receiving only his wrath eternally. As Romans 6:23 says, "The wages of sin is death." But the punishment for sin is not immediately felt. Instead, all mankind—regardless of whether they will ultimately receive God's grace or God's judgment—will continue to receive many blessings while on earth.

Sometimes those blessings will be physical. Jesus says in Matthew 5:45 that God "makes his sun rise on the evil and on the good, and sends rain on the just and on the unjust." The Creator of the universe sees to it that all people—those who believe in Jesus and those who have rejected his claims— receive from the abundance of his earth.

God's grace is also seen in the intellectual realm. Although Satan is "a liar and the father of lies" and "there is no truth in him" (John 8:44), even those who reject the claims of Jesus are not fully given over to falsehood and irrationality. Instead, many who clearly rejected God have made incredible discoveries and inventions. They did so not knowing that they were enlightened by Jesus, "the true light, which gives light to everyone" (John 1:9). When we benefit from these advancements, we are benefiting ultimately from God's common grace.

This common grace is seen in many other areas of life: the moral realm (people are not as evil as they could be), the creative realm (we can both produce and appreciate many different kinds of good and beautiful things), the societal realm (many communities, institutions, and governments protect and provide for their members and constituents), and even the religious realm (Jesus tells his followers in Matthew 5:44 to pray for their persecutors, showing that God answers many prayers that are prayed for the benefit of unbelievers).

Although common grace does not save people, God's delaying his judgment allows many to come to salvation: "The Lord is not slow to fulfill his promise as some count slowness, but is patient toward you, not wishing that any should perish, but that all should reach repentance" (2 Peter 3:9). Such common grace already demonstrates a large measure of God's goodness and mercy toward all mankind. His continual pouring out of blessings on all people will show him as just on the day of judgment when he finally punishes those who rejected him. Finally, as in all things, God's bestowing common grace on all people demonstrates his glory through their imitation of his character in their many activities. Therefore, we can appreciate and enjoy the manifestation of God's grace through all people, recognizing that ultimately God deserves the praise and glory for these blessings.

It's All Grace

The doctrine of election demonstrates to us that God loved us, not for who we are or what we have done or will do, but simply because he decided to love us. Therefore, our appropriate response to God is to give him praise for all eternity. Our appropriate response to others is humility since individually we have no claim on any portion of God's grace—it's all a gift from him.

Questions for Review and Application

1. How does your understanding of the doctrine of election cause you to rejoice? What troubles you about it?
2. In light of the doctrine of election, in what ways do our choices have meaning?
3. Can you name some specific ways in which you have recently seen God bless his creation through common grace? Take a moment to pray, thanking God for specific examples of the grace he has given to all people.

13

WHAT DOES IT MEAN TO BECOME A CHRISTIAN?

Paul sets forth an order in which the blessings of salvation come to Christians when he writes in Romans 8:30: "And those whom he predestined he also called, and those whom he called he also justified, and those whom he justified he also glorified." We dealt with predestination in the previous chapter; now, in the next four chapters, we will discuss the other aspects of this verse.

Effective Calling

The calling Paul refers to in Romans 8:30 is not the type of "calling" that people sometimes refer to when giving the reason they chose one job over another or chose to become a member of a certain church. Instead, this calling is related to those who were "predestined" and who became "justified." That is, it is a calling that came specifically to all who are believers in Jesus.

This kind of calling is a summons from the King of the universe; it is a summons that can't be denied, and it brings about the desired response in people's hearts. This calling is an act of God the Father, speaking through the human proclamation of the gospel, in which he summons people to himself in such a way that they respond in saving faith. Because it comes from God and always results in saving faith, it is sometimes referred to as *effective calling*.

When God calls people in this powerful way, he calls them "out of darkness into his marvelous light" (1 Peter 2:9); he calls them "into the fellowship of his Son" (1 Cor. 1:9; cf. Acts 2:39) and "into his own kingdom and glory" (1 Thess. 2:12; cf. 1 Peter 5:10; 2 Peter 1:3). People who have been called by God "belong to Jesus Christ" (Rom. 1:6). They are called to "be saints" (Rom. 1:7; 1 Cor. 1:2) and have come into a realm of peace (1 Cor. 7:15; Col. 3:15), freedom (Gal. 5:13), hope (Eph. 1:18; 4:4), holiness (1 Thess. 4:7), patient endurance of suffering (1 Peter 2:20–21; 3:9), and eternal life (1 Tim. 6:12).

General Calling and the Gospel Call

But there is a broader sense of "calling" that refers to any preaching of the gospel to anyone, whether they respond or not. In distinction from effective calling, which always brings response, we can talk about the "gospel call" in general, which goes forth to all people, and which is sometimes referred to as *external calling* or *general calling*.

The gospel call goes forth through the human preaching of the gospel. Paul makes this clear in 2 Thessalonians 2:14, when he writes to believers that their calling from God came through "our gospel"—that is, the gospel that Paul and others preached to them. That is why it is important that we boldly proclaim the gospel message, trusting that God will, through his effective call, do what he did with Lydia in Acts 16:14: "The Lord opened her heart to pay attention to what was said by Paul."

Not all gospel calls are effective. The job of believers is

to explain the gospel message; it is God's job to make that message or call effective.

Elements of the Gospel Call

There are three key elements that should be a part of every gospel call: an explanation of the facts concerning salvation; an invitation to respond to Christ personally in repentance and faith; and a promise of forgiveness and eternal life.

The facts concerning salvation are basically these:

1. All people have sinned (Rom. 3:23).
2. The penalty for our sin is death (Rom. 6:23).
3. Jesus Christ died to pay the penalty for our sins (Rom. 5:8).

But simply stating these facts isn't enough. There must be an invitation to repent and believe this good news personally. One such invitation, originally spoken by Jesus many years ago and found in Matthew 11:28–30, should still be heard as if Jesus were speaking it to you today: "Come to me, all who labor and are heavy laden, and I will give you rest. Take my yoke upon you, and learn from me, for I am gentle and lowly in heart, and you will find rest for your souls. For my yoke is easy, and my burden is light."

To those who respond in faith to the gospel call, God promises that their sins will be forgiven and that they will experience eternal life with God himself. "For God so loved the world, that he gave his only Son, that whoever believes in him should not perish but have eternal life" (John 3:16). As Jesus said in John 6:37, "Whoever comes to me I will never cast out."

How the Call Is Received

After the invitation to respond to the gospel is given, God must bring about a change in an individual's heart before he or she is able to respond in faith. That change, a secret act of God in which he imparts new spiritual life to us, is sometimes called regeneration. We play no role in this regeneration; it is completely an act of God.

This change of heart is described in Ezekiel 36:26: "And I will give you a new heart, and a new spirit I will put within you. And I will remove the heart of stone from your flesh and give you a heart of flesh."

This instantaneous event changes everything. Once it happens, recipients are, in the words of 2 Corinthians 5:17, "a new creation. The old has passed away . . . the new has come." This change, although not always immediately realized, results in a transformed heart that leads to a transformed character that produces a transformed life. All areas of life are changed. A regenerated individual should expect a new love for God and his people (Matt. 22:37–40), a heartfelt obedience to his commands (John 14:15), and the Christlike character traits Paul calls the fruit of the Spirit (Gal. 5:22–23).

How the Call Is Responded To

Once God has summoned through an effective call and changed a person's heart through regeneration, the necessary response is repentance and faith. But since the gospel call is a personal call, it requires a personal response. This willing, personal, individual response to the gospel call, in which a person sincerely repents of his sins and places his trust in Christ for salvation, is called conversion.

Simply knowing and affirming the facts of salvation as stated above in the gospel call is not enough. True saving faith, while it includes knowledge (knowing the facts of salvation) and approval (agreeing that the facts are true), also requires trust. Therefore, one who has true saving faith has moved from investigating Jesus' claims to believing that these claims are true and from believing these claims are true to personally trusting in Jesus for forgiveness of sins and eternal life with God. If I have true saving faith, I no longer simply believe facts about Jesus; instead, I personally trust Jesus to save *me*. The Bible uses strong language to describe this personal trust: we do not just have to "believe Jesus" (that is, believe that what he says is truthful), but we have to "believe in him" (that is, put personal trust in him and depend on him): "For God so loved the world, that he gave his only Son, that whoever *believes in him* should not perish but have eternal life" (John 3:16).

This trust involves two aspects: repentance and faith. Paul preached a gospel "of repentance toward God and of faith in our Lord Jesus Christ" (Acts 20:21). The author of Hebrews says that the first two elements of foundational Christian teaching are "repentance from dead works" and "faith toward God" (Heb. 6:1). Repentance means a conscious decision to turn away from your sins, and faith means turning to Christ to forgive those sins. This kind of faith is admitting that you can't save yourself and at the same time believing that Christ can.

Repentance and faith are really two sides of the same coin. For when I genuinely renounce and forsake my sin, I then turn in faith to Christ, trusting in him alone for my salvation. And this initial repentance and faith provides a pattern for ongoing heart attitudes of repentance and faith that continue for the rest of a Christian's life. As Paul writes in Colossians 2:6, "As you received Christ Jesus the Lord, so walk in him."

Questions for Review and Application

1. How does someone become a Christian?
2. Can you explain what it means to truly believe in Jesus? What does it mean to truly repent of sins?
3. In what ways can Christians give evidence of their belief in Jesus?

WHAT ARE JUSTIFICATION AND ADOPTION?

Paul writes in Romans 8:30 that those whom God called "he also justified." We discussed "calling" in the previous chapter. In this chapter we will discuss what God does after he effectively calls someone and after that person responds positively to God's call in repentance and saving faith.

Justification Is a Legal Declaration by God

When someone responds to God's call in repentance and faith, God responds to that faith by thinking of that person's sins as forgiven and by thinking of Christ's righteousness as belonging to that person. At that very moment God also declares that person to be righteous in his sight. This act of God is called "justification." Justification is an instantaneous legal act of God in which he (1) thinks of our sins as forgiven and thinks of Christ's righteousness as belonging to us and therefore (2) declares us to be "just" or morally righteous in his sight.

Paul is clear that this justification comes *after* we respond
to the gospel call in faith and that justification is God's
response to our faith. In Romans 3:26 Paul writes that God is
the "justifier of the one who has faith in Jesus," and in Romans
5:1 that we are "justified by faith." In Galatians 2:16 he writes,
"We know that a person is not justified by works of the law but
through faith in Jesus Christ." These verses clearly show that
justification is by faith.

(When James says a person is "justified by works" in
James 2:21, 24, and 25, he is not contradicting Paul; he is
using "justified" in a different sense, not meaning "declared
righteous by God," but "shown to be righteous before other
people," as is clear from the context of James 2:18–26, where
he talks about outward evidence that a person has faith.)

A Declaration That We Are
Righteous before God

Justification is a legal declaration by God; it is God acting as a
judge, declaring that an individual is righteous in his sight. If
God has declared you righteous in his sight, you do not have to
pay the penalty for your past, present, or future sins. As Paul
writes in Romans 8:1, "There is therefore now no condemnation for those who are in Christ Jesus." Later, in Romans 8:33,
Paul makes it clear that no one can bring a charge against or
condemn God's elect. Those whom God has justified have full
forgiveness of their sins.

The sins of those justified are considered forgiven because
God considers their sins as belonging to Christ, and Christ
already paid the penalty for those sins. But not only does God
consider those sins as belonging to Christ; he also considers
Christ's righteousness as belonging to us. Christ took the place

of guilt that we all deserved so that we could take the place of acceptance we all long for. As 2 Corinthians 5:21 says, "For our sake he made him to be sin who knew no sin, so that in him we might become the righteousness of God." Because of Christ's work on our behalf, God can, through justification, consider our sins as fully forgiven and consider us as fully acceptable and righteous in his sight.

Justification by Faith Alone

Paul explains that people are "justified" by God's grace "as a gift, through the redemption that is in Christ Jesus" (Rom. 3:24). In Ephesians 2:8–9 Paul is clear when he writes, "By grace you have been saved *through faith*. And this is not your own doing; it is the gift of God, not a result of works, so that no one may boast." Justification comes as a result of God's grace (which means we don't deserve it), and it comes as God's response to our faith (which is the opposite of depending on ourselves or our good works).

Although justification comes about as God's act in *response to* our faith, that does not mean our faith has any merit before God. It is not our faith that earns us favor with God. Scripture is clear: justification is based solely on the merits of Christ's work (see Rom. 3:24 above); it is never based on any merit in our faith. This really is wonderful news because it means we don't have to create value or make payment of sins for ourselves. We can look to God, through Christ, to freely give us that which we know we can't give ourselves.

The doctrine of justification was the central difference between Protestants and Roman Catholics at the time of the Reformation, which began with Martin Luther in Wittenberg, Germany, in 1517. Luther and all other Protestants who followed him insisted that justification was by "faith *alone*," while Roman Catholics responded that justification was by faith plus use of the "means of grace" found in the sacraments of the church (such as baptism, confirmation, the Eucharist or the Lord's Supper as experienced in the mass, and penance). The Protestant doctrine of justification says that we are fully justified by God the instant we believe, for "there is therefore now no condemnation for those who are in Christ Jesus" (Rom. 8:1). The Roman Catholic doctrine says that we are not fully justified until our lives are completely cleansed from sin, which will not be until after we die and we have been purified in purgatory (Protestants say there is no purgatory). These differences between Protestants and our Roman Catholic friends about justification have continued to this day.

Adoption: Membership in a New Family

In addition to justification, there is another privilege given to those who look to God for their salvation: God makes us members of his family. This act of God is called adoption.

Adoption differs from justification. It is dependent on justification, the legal declaration by God, acting as a judge, declaring an individual righteous in his sight, only because of the work of Jesus. Because of this legal declaration, God can count us as members of his family. Prior to God's act of justification, we only could receive God's wrath justly due to our sin. In the act of justification, God considers our sins as belonging to Christ (who paid the full penalty for those sins) and considers Christ's righteousness as belonging to us. It is because of Jesus' work for us (the atonement) and God's declaration about us (justification) that we can become part of God's family.

In John 1:12 we are told that to all who received Christ, to those "who believed in his name, he gave the right to become children of God." This is not a privilege available for everyone; Paul says in Ephesians 2:2–3 that those who don't believe in Christ are "sons of disobedience" and "children of wrath."

Because believers are considered children of God, we experience many of the benefits of adoption now. As children of God, we have the privilege of an intimate relationship with God, whom we can call our Father (Rom. 8:15). We do not have to live a fearful life of slavish obedience; instead, we are free to experience the joy of living as heirs to all the blessings that God desires to lavish upon his children (Rom. 8:15, 17).

We who are adopted by God experience some of the blessings and benefits of being his children now, but we will not experience these blessings fully until Christ returns. On the one hand, "we are God's children now" (1 John 3:2), but on the other hand, we "groan inwardly," waiting for the day when the full blessings of our adoption are experienced (Rom. 8:23).

In the interim the lives of God's children will be marked by much blessing but also by suffering (Rom. 8:17). These sufferings, Paul promises, "are not worth comparing with the glory that is to be revealed" at Christ's return (Rom. 8:18). That will be the day when God himself will wipe away "every tear" from his children's eyes and when death, mourning, crying, and pain "shall be no more" (Rev. 21:4).

Questions for Review and Application

1. What does it mean to be justified?
2. How are Christians justified? Do you really believe that you have been fully justified once for all time?
3. If you are a Christian, how does it make you feel to be part of God's family? Why does it make you feel this way? Can you name some of the specific blessings that come from adoption?

chapter

WHAT ARE SANCTIFICATION AND PERSEVERANCE?

As mentioned in chapter 13, conversion—repenting of our sins and trusting God for salvation—sets the pattern for the rest of Christian life. Repentance and faith result in justification; but repentance and faith also aid what is sometimes called *sanctification*. Sanctification is a progressive work of both God and man that makes Christians more and more free from sin and more and more like Christ in their actual lives. God and his children cooperate in this work, both playing distinct roles. And while Christians can expect to progress in their sanctification, they will never achieve perfection until Christ returns.

Sanctification Is a Process

Sanctification starts at the point of regeneration (God's gift of new spiritual life) and increases throughout life. At regeneration, Paul says, Christians are "set free from sin" (Rom. 6:18) and so must consider themselves "dead to sin and alive to God in Christ Jesus . . . for sin will have no dominion" over them

(Rom. 6:11, 14). This initial break from the power of sin means that Christians are no longer ruled or dominated by sin and no longer love to sin.

But since sanctification is a process, we will never be completely free from sin in this life. As 1 John 1:8 says, "If we say we have no sin, we deceive ourselves, and the truth is not in us." Or, as is written in Ecclesiastes 7:20, "Surely there is not a righteous man on earth who does good and never sins." Knowing this, Jesus commanded his disciples to pray (on what appears to be a daily basis), "forgive us our sins" (Luke 11:4).

Once Christians die and go to be with God, their sanctification is completed because their souls are set free from indwelling sin and made perfect. The author of Hebrews says that when we come into the presence of God to worship we come "to the spirits of the righteous made perfect" (Heb. 12:23). This is only appropriate because it is in anticipation of the fact that "nothing unclean will ever enter" into the presence of God (Rev. 21:27). But in another sense, sanctification, since it involves the whole person (body and soul), will not be complete until the Lord returns and he transforms "our lowly body to be like his glorious body" (Phil. 3:21). Then our bodies too will be made perfect and will be free from all the influences of sin. Although we will never be completely free from sin in this life, we should still expect to see a regular increase in our sanctification. Paul says that we "are being transformed . . . from one degree of glory to another" (2 Cor. 3:18). He also says, "Forgetting what lies behind and straining forward to what lies ahead, I press on toward the goal for the prize of the upward call of God in Christ Jesus" (Phil. 3:13–14). The picture is of a lifelong, continuous process. The Bible isn't specific on what amount of increase in sanctification we should expect in this life. It also doesn't tell us specifically what that increase will look like or what specific sins we will no longer struggle with. In fact, sometimes we will experience great freedom from one sin followed by deep struggle with another.

Yet, in all of this, Christians should never give up their struggle. They should never say that any one sin has defeated them. They should never say they cannot change. Instead, in the midst of the struggle, they should cling to the promises of God, like the one found in Romans 6:14: "Sin will have no dominion over you."

God's Role in Sanctification

Sanctification is primarily the work of God. Paul indicates this when he prays in 1 Thessalonians 5:23, "May the God of peace himself sanctify you completely." The author of Hebrews affirms this when he writes, "May the God of peace . . . equip you with everything good that you may do his will, working in us that which is pleasing in his sight, through Jesus Christ, to whom be glory forever and ever" (Heb. 13:20–21).

God equips his children through the power of the Holy Spirit. The Holy Spirit is the one who works within us to change and sanctify us, giving us greater holiness in life. That is why Peter speaks of the "sanctification of the Spirit" in 1 Peter 1:2, and why Paul speaks of the "sanctification by the Spirit" in 2 Thessalonians 2:13. It is the Holy Spirit who produces in us the "fruit of the Spirit" (Gal. 5:22–23), those character traits that are part of greater and greater sanctification. As we grow in sanctification, we "walk by the Spirit" and are "led by the Spirit" (Gal. 5:16–18), that is, we are more and more responsive to the desires and promptings of the Holy Spirit in our life and character. The Holy Spirit is the spirit of holiness; therefore he produces holiness within us.

Our Role in Sanctification

We are both passively and actively involved in sanctification. Through repentance and faith we are told to present ourselves "to God as those who have been brought from death to life" (Rom. 6:13). This is our passive involvement. But we are also told in Romans 8:13 to "put to death the deeds of the body" (that is, sin), which implies an active role on our part. Although Paul clearly says we are only able to do so by the power of the Spirit (Rom. 8:13), we are nevertheless told that we have an active role.

The same active and passive role is found in Philippians 2:12–13: "Work out your own salvation with fear and trembling, for it is God who works in you, both to will and to work for his good pleasure." The encouragement to work out our own salvation is based on the promise that God will work in us—God will empower our work! For this very reason, those who believe in Jesus can confidently "strive . . . for the holiness without which no one will see the Lord" (Heb. 12:14).

Becoming a Christian is a gift from God that requires our involvement; we find the same to be true for sanctification. Progress in sanctification is a gift of grace, but it is a gift we can expect to receive. Just as God honors our initial faith (faith that he gives us), he also honors our continual acts of faith and obedience, seen through Bible reading and meditation (Ps. 1:2; Matt. 4:4; John 17:17), prayer (Eph. 6:18; Phil. 4:6), worship (Eph. 5:18–20), witnessing (Matt. 28:19–20), acts of mercy and justice (Matt. 23:23; James 1:27), Christian fellowship (Heb. 10:24–25), and self-discipline or self-control (Gal. 5:23; Titus 1:8).

It is important that we continue to grow both in our passive trust in God to sanctify us and in our active striving for holiness and obedience in our lives. If we neglect actively striving to obey God, we become lazy Christians. If we neglect the passive role of trusting God and yielding to him, we become proud and overly confident in ourselves. In either case our sanctification will be deficient. And if our sanctification is deficient, we won't experience the joy and peace promised to us (Gal. 5:22; Rom. 14:17).

What If the Sanctification Process Ends?

All true Christians should expect growth in sanctification during their lifetimes. But what if that process seems to end? And if it ends, what does that mean? Does it mean that we who once were Christians are now no longer Christians? All these questions have one final question at their root: can we really lose the blessings of our salvation?

The answer to that question is no. All who are truly Christians will be kept by God's power and will persevere as Christians until the end of their lives. But how do we know if we are truly Christians? What if some fall away from any profession of faith and live a life of active rebellion against God? With respect to such cases, we have to say that only those who persevere until the end are truly Christians. This two-part teaching (all true Christians will persevere, and only those who persevere are true Christians) is sometimes referred to as the *perseverance of the saints.*

The Promise of Jesus

First, there is scriptural evidence that all true Christians will persevere. In John 6:38–40 Jesus says: "I have come down from heaven, not to do my own will but the will of him who sent me. And this is the will of him who sent me, that I should lose nothing of all that he has given me, but raise it up on the last day. For this is the will of my Father, that everyone who looks on the Son and believes in him should have eternal life, and I will raise him up on the last day."

Here Jesus says that everyone who believes in him will have eternal life. He says that he will raise that person up at the last day, giving that person eternal life with him. Moreover, Jesus says it is God's will that he "lose nothing" of all God has given him.

Jesus makes a similar promise in John 10:27–29: "My sheep hear my voice, and I know them, and they follow me. I give them eternal life, and they will never perish, and no one will snatch them out of my hand. My Father, who has given them to me, is greater than all, and no one is able to snatch them out of the Father's hand."

In John 10:28 specifically, Jesus says two things about his followers. First, he says, "No one will snatch them out of my hand." Second, he says, "they will never perish." These phrases, taken together, drive home the wonderful promise that those to whom Jesus gives eternal life will never lose that life.

These are just two of the promises given by Jesus regarding the perseverance of the saints. From these two passages, it seems clear that Jesus understood that those who received eternal life from him would keep that eternal life for all eternity.

The Promise of the Holy Spirit

Further evidence that God keeps Christians safe for eternity is the seal that he places upon us. The seal is the Holy Spirit within us. Paul, in Ephesians 1:13–14, writes that when we first believed in Jesus, we "were sealed with the promised Holy Spirit, who is the guarantee of our inheritance until we acquire possession of it, to the praise of his glory." The inheritance promised by God includes all the further blessings of eternal life and a great reward in heaven with him. The seal, or guarantee, of that promise is God's very presence—the Holy Spirit—present in every Christian.

The Promise in Perseverance

While those who are truly Christians will persevere to the end, only those who persevere to the end are truly Christians. In John 8:31, Jesus says, "If you abide in my word, you are truly my disciples." That is, one evidence of genuine faith is continuing to believe and obey what Jesus said and commanded.

Paul, in Colossians 1:22–23, writes to the Christians there that Christ reconciled them to God "in order to present you holy and blameless and above reproach before him, if indeed you continue in the faith, stable and steadfast, not shifting from the hope of the gospel that you heard." Not wanting to give those who weren't truly Christians a false assurance, Paul put a condition of perseverance on the promise he was giving. By saying, "if indeed you continue in the faith," Paul is not trying to threaten or scare true believers; instead, he is saying that those who don't truly believe will eventually fall away from the faith they claim to have.

The promise in perseverance is that those who continue in faith until the end of their lives are true Christians. As we stated earlier, this does not mean these people will live perfect lives. True Christians may have deep struggles with sin at different times in their lives. But what it does mean is that those struggles will actually be struggles. True Christians will fight against sin through repentance and faith. The promise in perseverance serves as a warning to those who aren't truly

Christians because it gives them reason to believe that if they do fall or have fallen away from the faith, it is a strong indication that they were never true believers in the first place.

Assurance of Perseverance

The author of Hebrews tells us one way to know that our faith in Christ is genuine is by holding our "original confidence firm to the end" (Heb. 3:14). Yet if the *only* confidence we have that our faith is genuine comes at the end of life, then we have little hope for today. We would always be wondering if we might fall away at the end of our lives and show that we weren't really saved. That kind of worry is not consistent with how the New Testament views our assurance.

In fact, true Christians can gain real assurance of salvation from other factors and especially from a present trust in Christ and his ongoing work in their lives. Our present trust in Christ for salvation is one assurance of true conversion. This is the teaching of the most famous verse in the Bible: "For God so loved the world, that he gave his only Son, that *whoever believes in him* should not perish but have eternal life" (John 3:16). If you believe in him, you have eternal life. If you have confidence in Christ's work on your behalf, confidence in Christ's ability to take the penalty for your sins and confidence that Christ should let you into heaven based only on his work and not on yours, and if that confidence is currently present in your life, then that confidence is an assurance of your true faith.

But a present trust in Christ for salvation is not the only thing that provides assurance. Evidence of an ongoing work of God in your life also provides assurance. This ongoing work will include the subjective testimony of the Holy Spirit in your heart, letting you know you are one of God's children

(1 John 4:13). It will also include the work of the Holy Spirit leading you in obedience to God's will (Rom. 8:14). And it will be shown by a life of "love, joy, peace, patience, kindness, goodness, faithfulness, gentleness, [and] self-control" (Gal. 5:22–23). While these won't always be perfectly evident, a survey of your life should show evidence of growth in these areas.

In addition, there should be evidence of a continuing, present relationship with Jesus Christ. For "whoever says 'I know him' but does not keep his commandments is a liar, and the truth is not in him, but whoever keeps his word, in him truly the love of God is perfected. By this we may know that we are in him: whoever says he abides in him ought to walk in the same way in which he walked" (1 John 2:4–6). A perfect life is not necessary, but a true Christian's life will continue to show a general pattern of obedience to Christ's commands and an imitation of his life.

This ongoing work of the Holy Spirit within us will be seen over a long period of time in our lives. That is, true Christians will grow in their sanctification. Peter tells us that one way to "confirm [our] calling and election" (2 Peter 1:10) is to increase our virtue, knowledge, self-control, steadfastness, godliness, brotherly affection, and love (2 Peter 1:5–8). Peter says if these qualities increase in our lives, we "will never fall" (2 Peter 1:10). If you sense these qualities lacking, do not simply try to replicate them in your life to bolster your assurance, but instead repent of their lack in your life and ask the Lord to give you growth in these areas.

Persevering through the Process

Sanctification is a lifelong process. If you are a believer in Jesus, at times it will seem as if the process is going at a faster rate than you ever thought possible. It's at these times that you will need to guard against pride and self-righteousness (thinking yourself better than you are and taking credit for your goodness that is really a gift of grace).

At other times, you will wonder if there is any life inside you at all. It's at these times that you may wonder if you are even truly a Christian. When such doubts begin to fill your thoughts, pray the prayer found in Mark 9:24: "I believe; help my unbelief!"

And in the midst of it all, hold sure to the promise that "by God's power" you "are being guarded through faith for a salvation ready to be revealed in the last time" (1 Peter 1:5). And take confidence in Jesus' statement that "this is the will of my Father, that everyone who looks on the Son and believes in him should have eternal life, and I will raise him up on the last day" (John 6:40).

Questions for Review and Application

1. How is sanctification different from justification?
2. What is our role in sanctification? What is God's role? What are some specific ways in which you could contribute more to your sanctification in the coming week?
3. List some passages of Scripture that support the doctrine of perseverance. As you reflect on those passages, how do they make you feel? Why do they make you feel that way?

16

WHAT IS DEATH?

A s mentioned in chapter 15, death brings a completion to one part of a Christian's sanctification. At death a Christian's soul is immediately made perfect and enters into the presence of God. But it isn't until Christ returns that Christians experience full perfection for both body and soul, for at that time their bodies will be raised and made perfect as well. In this chapter we will investigate what happens at both events, as well as what happens in between death and the time when Christ returns.

Why Do Christians Die?

Death is not a punishment for Christians. As was made clear in the previous four chapters, there is "no condemnation for those who are in Christ Jesus" (Rom. 8:1). The complete penalty for a Christian's sin has been paid by Christ Jesus.

Yet God, in his wisdom, decided it best that Christians not experience all the benefits of salvation at once. For example, Christians still sin, get sick, suffer from natural disasters, and fall prey to acts of evil and injustice. And Christians still die. All of these are the results of living in a world that isn't quite right, a world that isn't fully free from the curse of sin.

Paul tells us that although Christ defeated death when he rose from the dead, death will be the last result of sin to be removed from this fallen world: Christ "must reign until he has put all his enemies under his feet. The last enemy to be destroyed is death" (1 Cor. 15:25–26).

God uses the experience of death to complete our sanctification. God uses death as a means to make us more like Christ. In fact, in the Christian life generally it is not unusual for God to use hardship and pain to bring about good. Paul tells us in Romans 8:28, "We know that for those who love God all things work together for good." Pain and hardship are sometimes the result of God disciplining his children, "for the Lord disciplines the one he loves. . . . He disciplines us for our good, that we may share his holiness. For the moment all discipline seems painful rather than pleasant, but later it yields the peaceful fruit of righteousness to those who have been trained by it" (Heb. 12:6, 10–11).

Not all discipline serves to correct us when we have done wrong. Often God's discipline in our lives is a way of strengthening us; it is a means of sanctification. Although Jesus never sinned, he still "learned obedience through what he suffered" (Heb. 5:8) and was made "perfect through suffering" (Heb. 2:10). As he grew from childhood to adulthood and continued through his life on earth, the task of obedience to God became harder and harder, and it included much suffering. Through all of this, Jesus increased in his strength to obey.

Since God works even through our experience of death to complete our sanctification, preserving our life and general comfort is not our highest goal. Obedience to God and faithfulness in every circumstance is far more important. That is why Paul could tell the Ephesian elders, "I do not account my life of any value nor as precious to myself, if only I may finish my course and the ministry that I received from the Lord Jesus, to testify to the gospel of the grace of God" (Acts 20:24).

Even though God uses a hardship like death for a positive means in our life, it is important to remember that death is not merely "natural," as people without God's Word often think of it. Neither is sickness or evil or injustice natural. These things are not right, and in God's world they ought not to be. Although we live with these things now, one day all of them— even death—will finally be destroyed (1 Cor. 15:24–26).

When Christians Die

If you are a believer in Jesus, the Bible encourages you not to view your own death with fear. Jesus died to "deliver all those who through fear of death were subject to lifelong slavery" (Heb. 2:15). Instead, you are to view your own death with joy, knowing that after death you will be with Christ. Paul demonstrates a clear understanding of this in 2 Corinthians 5:8 when he writes, "We would rather be away from the body and at home with the Lord." He writes something similar in Philippians 1:23: "My desire is to depart and be with Christ, for that is far better."

If you fear death and find the words of Paul hard to believe, it may be helpful for you to confess that to the Lord. Ask him to increase your understanding of what happens when you die and to increase your faith in his goodness.

When Christians die, their souls go immediately into God's presence. Although their bodies remain in the ground, their souls go into the presence of their Creator. That is why Paul writes of being away from the body through death (2 Cor. 5:8) and departing in death to be with Christ (Phil. 1:23). Because the souls of Christians are eternally happy in the presence of God, there is no need to pray for them once they are dead. (This is an area where Roman Catholics hold a different view from Protestants, since they mistakenly believe that Christians who die go to purgatory and that our prayers can help them get out of purgatory sooner.)

Although we know that the souls of believers are eternally happy in the presence of God, it is still right that we feel sorrow at the death of a Christian friend or relative. When the apostle Stephen was stoned, "devout men . . . made great lamentation over him" (Acts 8:2). Jesus himself wept at the tomb of his friend Lazarus (John 11:35), both because of sorrow that his friend had died and because of sorrow for all who would experience the pain of death until his return.

But the sorrow felt at the death of a Christian is not a hopeless sorrow for we know that a believer has gone to be with the Lord. Paul writes in 1 Thessalonians 4:13 that we do not "grieve as others do who have no hope."

When Non-Christians Die

When people who have rejected the claims of Christ die, their souls go immediately to eternal punishment. But their bodies remain in the ground until Christ's return, when they will join their souls for the final day of judgment (see Matt. 25:31–46; John 5:28–29; Acts 24:15; and Rev. 20:12). Scripture never encourages us to think that people will have a second chance to trust in Christ after death. In fact, the situation is quite the contrary, as shown both in the parable of the rich man and Lazarus (see Luke 16:24–26) and in general statements about death and judgment (see Heb. 9:27: "It is appointed for man to die once, and after that comes judgment").

Therefore, the sorrow felt at the death of someone who

we believe has rejected Christ is not a sorrow mingled with hope. When Paul thought about some fellow Jews who had rejected Christ, he said, "I have great sorrow and unceasing anguish in my heart" (Rom. 9:2). However, we often do not have complete certainty that a friend or loved one has continued to reject Christ until the very end. The knowledge of impending death can bring about genuine heart searching, and a person may come to genuine repentance and faith. In some cases, we simply do not know. Nevertheless, after a non-Christian has died, it would be wrong to give any indication to others that we think the person has gone to heaven, for this would diminish the sense of urgency for those still alive to trust in Christ. When a non-Christian has died, it is often helpful to speak with genuine thankfulness about the good qualities that we noticed in the life of that person just as King David did when he learned that King Saul had died (2 Sam. 1:19–25).

When Are Christians Raised from the Dead?

Again, if you are a believer in Jesus, when you die, your body will remain in the ground and your soul will go immediately into the presence of God. And so, until Christ returns, we wait for "the redemption of our bodies. For in this hope we were saved" (Rom. 8:23–24). That will be the day, Paul says, when we will be "glorified with" Christ (Rom. 8:17).

For Christians who have died, the day when Christ returns will be the final step in the application of redemption. On that day their new, perfect bodies will be reunited with their souls. Christ was the first one raised with such a resurrection body, but Paul says that "at his coming" believers will also be raised in this way (1 Cor. 15:22–23). And for Christians who are still alive when Christ returns, their imperfect bodies will suddenly be changed into perfect ones. Paul says, "We shall not all sleep [that is, die], but we shall all be changed, in a moment, in the twinkling of an eye, at the last trumpet. For the trumpet will sound, and the dead will be raised imperishable, and we shall be changed" (1 Cor. 15:51–52). Therefore, all believers in Jesus will receive renewed resurrection bodies just like their Savior received (1 Cor. 15:20, 23, 49; Phil. 3:21). This process is called "glorification" since our bodies receive a new heavenly kind of glory.

These new bodies will be "imperishable" (1 Cor. 15:52), that is, they will not wear out, grow old, or ever be subject to sickness or disease. They will show no sign of aging but will instead be completely healthy and strong forever. The new bodies will be what God originally designed them to be: far more beautiful and attractive than anything we might imagine in this age. Those who are raised with Christ will forever live in bodies that have all the excellent qualities God created us to have. These bodies will forever be the living proof of the wisdom of God in creation—a creation he called "very good" (Gen. 1:31).

Questions for Review and Application

1. Why do Christians die? How does that affect the way you think about your own death someday?

2. What happens to the bodies and what happens to the souls of Christians when they die? How does this make you feel? Why does it make you feel this way?

3. What will happen to the bodies of Christians when Jesus returns to earth? What specific aspects of our resurrection bodies are you especially hopeful about?

17

WHAT IS THE CHURCH?

The church is the community of all true believers for all time. That is, the church is made up of all the men and women who have been, are, or ever will be true believers in Jesus. When Paul wrote in Ephesians 5:25 that "Christ loved the church and gave himself up for her," he was referring to all the people Christ died to redeem. He didn't just mean those who were alive after Christ had died but also those who looked to God for their salvation before Christ even came to earth. All true believers, regardless of what time period they lived in, make up the true church.

Jesus said that he would build his church (Matt. 16:18) by calling people to himself. This pattern of church building is a continuation of the process of building the church before Christ came to earth, for in Old Testament times God was continually calling his people to himself to be a worshiping assembly before him. Just as the whole nation of Israel in the Old Testament was to assemble together to worship God, so Christians today are called to do the same.

The Invisible Yet Visible Church

Because we cannot see the spiritual condition of people's hearts, the true church, in its spiritual reality as the fellowship of all genuine believers, is invisible. Only God can see the condition of people's hearts. As Paul says in 2 Timothy 2:19, "The Lord knows those who are his." Therefore, the "invisible church" is the church as God sees it. But the church is also visible. While the invisible church is the church as God sees it, the "visible church" is the church as Christians on earth see it. Therefore, the visible church will contain genuine believers as well as others who do not truly believe or follow the claims of Jesus. But in making this distinction, we should not become overly suspicious regarding the status of those who appear to be true believers. Instead, with benevolent judgment, we should consider all to be members of the universal church who appear to be believers from their confession of faith and their pattern of life.

Other Descriptions of the Church

In the New Testament, the word *church* is used to describe different types of groups of believers: a small house church (Rom. 16:5; 1 Cor. 16:19), the church in an entire city (1 Cor. 1:2; 2 Cor. 1:1; 1 Thess. 1:1), the church in an entire region (Acts 9:31), and the church throughout the entire world (Eph. 5:25; 1 Cor. 12:28). Therefore, a community of God's people at any level is rightly called a church.

A variety of metaphors are also used to describe the church. One group of metaphors suggests that the church is a family and that the members of the church relate to one another as members of a larger family do. This is why Paul writes in 1 Timothy 5:1–2, "Do not rebuke an older man but encourage him as you would a father, younger men as brothers, older women as mothers, younger women as sisters, in all purity." The relationship between Christ and the church is also seen in familial terms, with Christ as the groom and the church as his bride (Eph. 5:32; 2 Cor. 11:2).

Another common image of the church is that of a body. In 1 Corinthians 12 Paul refers to members of the church as members of one body. Members have their own special function and responsibility just like parts of the body do. In Ephesians 1:22–23; 4:15–16; and Colossians 2:19, the church is referred to as a body with Christ as its head, holding the entire body together and equipping every part to work as it should.

There are many other metaphors used for the church, such as a new temple (1 Peter 2:4–8), a holy priesthood (1 Peter 2:5), branches on a vine (John 15:5), an olive tree (Rom. 11:17–24), and a field of crops (1 Cor. 3:6–9). The wide range of metaphors used for the church should remind us not to focus too much on any one. An unbalanced emphasis on one metaphor to the exclusion of others will result in an unbalanced view of the church. Instead, we should consider each metaphor as a different perspective on the church, something that tells us a little more about the community of which God has allowed us to be a part.

What Makes a Church a Church?

If a group of people meet together to discuss spiritual things, does that make them a church? What if they do so in a church building as opposed to a coffee shop? What if, in addition to discussion, they sing and pray together? What if they add Bible reading to their group time? What activities make a church a church?

Traditionally, many Christian writers have agreed that there are two major activities (or "marks") that every church must exhibit in order to be truly considered a church. The first is correct preaching from the Bible. This mark has less to do

with the form of the sermon than with the content of the sermon. If the sermons in a church continually contain false doctrine or conceal the true gospel message of salvation by faith
alone, then the church in which those sermons are preached is
not a true church.

The second mark of a true church is the correct administration of the sacraments (or "ordinances"), which are baptism
and the Lord's Supper. Once an organization begins to practice
baptism and the Lord's Supper in a biblical way, then that
organization is functioning as a church. The practice of the two
sacraments is considered a mark of a true church because the
sacraments can serve as membership controls for the church;
that is, baptism is a means for admitting individuals into the
church, and partaking of the Lord's Supper is a way those
members continue to show their good standing within the
church body. Therefore, historically, many writers have said
that only those churches that properly practice the sacraments
are considered true churches.

But with so many parachurch organizations today (that is,
special ministries such as mission agencies, university Christian
groups, and Christian colleges), it is helpful to add another
"mark" of a true church: in order to be a church, an organization should be attempting to function as a church, rather than
encouraging its members to become part of a local church.

Among true churches, two further distinctions—as
emphasized in the New Testament—can be made. A church
can be more or less pure and more or less unified. The purity of
the church is determined by its degree of freedom from wrong
doctrine and conduct and its degree of conformity to God's
revealed will for the church. Christ's goal for the church is "that
he might sanctify her, having cleansed her by the washing of
water with the word, so that he might present the church to

himself in splendor, without spot or wrinkle or any such thing, that she might be holy and without blemish" (Eph. 5:26–27). Therefore, as members of the church, we should pursue its purity in all areas to the best of our ability.

In addition, we should also pursue unity—that is, freedom from divisions among true Christians—to the best of our ability. When we do this, we are falling in line with Jesus' prayer in John 17:21 for future believers "that they may all be one." This does not mean that there must be one worldwide church government over all Christians, for unity can be manifested in other ways. It does, however, mean that every true church should try to cooperate and affiliate with other true churches and Christian groups in various appropriate ways from time to time. Churches that tend to be constantly in disagreement with most other churches should prayerfully consider how well they are working toward Christ's goal of unity among believers.

What Is the Church Supposed to Do?

The church is supposed to minister to God, to its members, and to the world. Ministry to God is done through worshiping him. In Colossians 3:16 Paul encourages the church to sing "psalms and hymns and spiritual songs, with thankfulness in your hearts to God." Worship in the church is not merely a preparation for something else; it is in itself a fulfillment of a major purpose of the church, whose members were created to live for the praise of God's glory (Eph. 1:12).

The church's ministry to its members is done through nurturing and building them up so that the church can "present everyone mature in Christ" (Col. 1:28). As Paul said in Ephesians 4:12–13, the church's gifted leaders were given "to equip the saints for the work of ministry, for building up the body of Christ, until we all attain to the unity of the faith and of the knowledge of the Son of God, to mature manhood, to the measure of the stature of the fullness of Christ."

The church's ministry to the world is done through preaching the gospel to all people in word and in deed. In Matthew 28:19 Jesus commands his disciples to "make disciples of all nations." In Acts 1:8 the disciples were told to spread the gospel message "to the end of the earth." And the pattern of preaching in Scripture is clear: the message is to be given in both word (through evangelism) and deed (through ministries of mercy).

Each church should be involved in various kinds of ministries of word and deed, including not only evangelism but also ministry to the poor and oppressed (Gal. 2:10; James 1:27). And while there seems to be a primacy placed on caring for the physical needs of fellow believers (Acts 11:29; 2 Cor. 8:4; 1 John 3:17), all members of the church, as they have opportunity, are to "do good to everyone" (Gal. 6:10).

Every church should attempt to fulfill the three purposes God created it for (worship, nurture, and evangelism and mercy). One purpose is not more important than the other, and no church should seek to make one purpose primary to the neglect of the others. Instead, with the full confidence in Christ's promise that he will build his church (Matt. 16:18), every church should wholeheartedly seek to worship God, build its members to maturity, and preach the good news of the gospel to the world through word and deed.

The Church's Power to Fulfill Its Mission

When Christ promised to build his church, he gave his disciples the authority to do so. And when he left them, he sent them the Holy Spirit to empower them to build it (John 14:26; Acts 1:8). The Holy Spirit empowered Jesus' followers with the gifts ("spiritual gifts") required to do the ministry of the church, and the Holy Spirit empowers us to use these gifts to continue the ministry of the church today.

Spiritual gifts include both gifts related to natural ability (teaching, showing mercy, administration) and gifts that appear to be more miraculous (prophecy, healing, distinguishing between spirits). Although some may make a distinction between the natural and miraculous gifts, when Paul lists spiritual gifts, he doesn't seem to make such a distinction (Rom. 12:6–8; 1 Cor. 7:7; 12:8–10, 28; Eph. 4:11). Nor does he seem to say that some of the more miraculous gifts were only given to the apostles as signs to authenticate their early ministry, for these gifts were widely distributed among believers in the various churches at Paul's time. But Paul says in 1 Corinthians 13:12 that the more miraculous gifts will pass away (see v. 10) when we see Christ "face to face" and when we "know fully." When Christ returns, spiritual gifts will pass away, for there will no longer be any need for them (1 Cor. 13:8).

All spiritual gifts, Paul says in 1 Corinthians 12:11, are "empowered by one and the same Spirit, who apportions to each one individually as he wills." These gifts are given "for the common good" (1 Cor. 12:7) and are to be used for "building up" the church (1 Cor. 14:26). Not only do spiritual gifts equip the church for the ministry to which it is called, but they also give the world a foretaste of the age to come. When Christ returns, his rule and reign over all the earth will be fully known and experienced, not only in the sinless lives of individuals (1 John 3:2) but also in the glorified bodies of believers (1 Cor. 15:53). As the church, through the power of the Spirit, makes this future promise a present reality (for example, through the conversion of an unbeliever or the healing of sickness), it is giving all who will see a taste of what is to come and fulfilling the mission Christ commanded and empowered it to fulfill.

Questions for Review and Application

1. How is a church different from a Bible study or Christian retreat?
2. Why should Christians become members of a church? What are some of the dangers of not becoming a member of a local church?
3. Can you list some of the things a church is supposed to do? Can you name some specific examples of the Holy Spirit's work empowering and blessing some of those things in your own church?

chapter

18

WHAT WILL HAPPEN WHEN CHRIST RETURNS?

There have been many debates in the history of the church over questions regarding the future. Specifically, the debates have centered on the return of Christ, the millennium (or "thousand years"), the final judgment, the eternal punishment of unbelievers and eternal reward of believers, and life with God in the new heaven and new earth. Studies of these events are called studies of the "last things," or "eschatology" (from the Greek *eschatos*, meaning "last").

The Return of Christ

Jesus told his disciples that he would return to earth a second time: "I will come again and will take you to myself, that where I am you may be also" (John 14:3). While it is clear from this and other passages (such as Acts 1:11; 1 Thess. 4:16; Heb. 9:28; 2 Peter 3:10; 1 John 3:2) that Jesus himself will return, these passages also make it clear that "no one knows" (Mark 13:32) the exact time of that return, for "the Son of Man is coming at an hour you do not expect" (Matt. 24:44).

Although no one can know the time of Christ's return,

all believers should respond as John did in Revelation 22:20 when he heard Christ say, "Surely I am coming soon." John's response was "Amen. Come, Lord Jesus!"

The Timing of the Return

While the verses cited above are clear that Christ's return will come at a time that no one knows, other passages in the Bible seem to suggest that certain signs will precede the time of Christ's return. These signs, as shown through the verses that support them, are as follows:

- "The gospel must first be proclaimed to all nations" (Mark 13:10; see also Matt. 24:14).
- "There will be such tribulation as has not been from the beginning of the creation that God created until now, and never will be. And if the Lord had not cut short the days, no human being would be saved. But for the sake of the elect, whom he chose, he shortened the days" (Mark 13:19–20).
- "False christs and false prophets will arise and perform signs and wonders, to lead astray, if possible, the elect" (Mark 13:22; see also Matt. 24:23–24).
- "After that tribulation, the sun will be darkened, and the moon will not give its light, and the stars will be falling from heaven, and the powers in the heavens will be shaken" (Mark 13:24–25; see also Matt. 24:29–30; Luke 21:25–27).
- "Now concerning the coming of our Lord Jesus Christ . . . that day will not come, unless the rebellion comes first, and the man of lawlessness is revealed, the son of destruction, who opposes and exalts himself

against every so-called god or object of worship, so that he takes his seat in the temple of God, proclaiming himself to be God" (2 Thess. 2:1, 3–4).

• "I do not want you to be unaware of this mystery. . . . All Israel will be saved" (Rom. 11:25–26).

Jesus did not say these signs were given so that people would think that since they haven't seen the signs, Christ couldn't return. Instead, they were given to intensify an expectation of Christ's return: "Now when these things begin to take place, straighten up and raise your heads, because your redemption is drawing near" (Luke 21:28).

But the mentioning of these signs raises two legitimate questions: Have any of these signs occurred? And, if they haven't all occurred, could Christ really return at any moment? The answers to these questions vary throughout the church.

Some believe these signs haven't occurred and therefore Christ won't return at any moment. But Jesus encouraged his disciples, "Be on guard, keep awake. For you do not know when the time will come" (Mark 13:33). A view that tells Christians that Christ cannot return soon seems to nullify the force of Christ's encouragement. It also incorrectly assumes that those who hold this view rightly understand what the signs will look like and rightly know all that has happened in the world that might fulfill these signs.

Others believe that Christ could indeed come at any time, and they deal with the fulfillment of the signs in three distinct ways. (1) Some argue that there will be two separate comings of Christ: a secret return and a public return. But the passages that speak of his return don't seem to support two separate returns (see discussion below).

(2) Others argue that all the signs were already fulfilled in the early history of the church and that therefore Christ could really return at any moment. But some of the signs (for example, the great tribulation, the salvation of Israel, the appearance of the "man of lawlessness," and the stars falling from heaven) do not seem to have been fulfilled in any clear or evident way at the time of the early church. (3) Still others argue that it is *unlikely but possible* that the signs have been fulfilled and that therefore Christ could return at any moment.

In light of the ambiguity related to the fulfillment of these signs, it seems that the last view is the most reasonable. This view allows us to expect that the signs preceding Christ's return will probably still happen in the future, but since we are somewhat unsure about that, we can still be ready for Christ to suddenly return any day. (On this view, being ready for Christ's return is somewhat similar to wearing a seat belt in a car: you do not think that you will get in an accident, but you still wear the seat belt because you might be wrong.)

The Events at the Return

Much of the disagreement within the church regarding Jesus' return deals directly with the interpretation of one Bible passage: Revelation 20:1–6. Specifically, the disagreement has to do with the thousand years that John mentions in Revelation 20:4–5 when he writes that certain people "came to life and reigned with Christ for a thousand years. The rest of the dead did not come to life until the thousand years were ended." Many Christians term this thousand-year stage "the millennium," and they usually take one of three views on the time and nature of this period.

View 1—Amillennial: The millennium is now, and when it ends, Jesus will return

The simplest view of the millennium is that Revelation 20:1–6 describes not a future time but the present church age. Christians who hold to this view believe that many or all of the previously mentioned signs occurred early on in church history and that Christ could really return at any moment. According to this view, when John writes that "they came to life and reigned with Christ for a thousand years" (Rev. 20:4), he means that Christians who have already died are today reigning with Christ in a spiritual sense (see Matthew 28:18 where Jesus said, "All authority in heaven and on earth has been given to me," and Ephesians 2:6, which says that we are seated with Christ "in the heavenly places"). Since the events in Revelation 20 are currently being fulfilled in the church, the thousand-year period John mentions in Revelation 20:4–5 is a figure of speech for a long period of time—namely, the entire church age from Pentecost until Christ's return.

This view would say that Satan, who in Revelation 20:2–3 is said to be "bound" and sealed in a pit "so that he might not deceive the nations any longer," had his power significantly reduced during Christ's ministry on earth (Matt. 12:28–29; Luke 10:18). The fact that someone like Paul could teach all Gentile nations about "the Lord Jesus Christ with all boldness and without hindrance" (Acts 28:31) is a demonstration that Satan has been "bound" so that he does not "deceive the nations any longer."

This view is often called the amillennial view, because those who hold to it don't believe that Revelation 20:4–5 teaches a future thousand-year reign either before or after Jesus' return. Instead, they believe that when Christ returns, there will be one resurrection of both believers and unbelievers.

Those who believe in Jesus will go to heaven; those who don't will face the final judgment and eternal condemnation. At that time the new heavens and new earth will begin and remain for eternity. One argument in favor of this view is that it is all very simple and uncomplicated: Christ returns, judgment takes place, and we live in the new heavens and new earth forever.

View 2—Postmillennial: The millennium will come gradually, and Jesus will return after the millennium

Other Christians believe Jesus will return after the thousand years mentioned in Revelation 20:4–5. As the church grows and Christians continue to have a greater and greater influence, society will begin to function more and more in line with God's standards. Gradually, a "millennial age" of great peace and righteousness (not necessarily a literal one thousand years) will come about on the earth. Christ will not physically reign on earth during this period; instead, Christians will have a tremendous influence in society, and Christ's reign will come about through this influence of Christians. People who support this view emphasize verses that show how the kingdom of God grows quietly but steadily from a tiny start to a huge end. For example, there is the parable of the mustard seed that became a great tree (Matt. 13:31–32) and Jesus' statement that "the kingdom of heaven is like leaven that a woman took and hid in three measures of flour, till it was all leavened" (Matt. 13:33). Postmillennialists also emphasize Jesus' statement, "All authority in heaven and on earth has been given to me" (Matt. 28:18), and they expect that as a result the kingdom of God will continue to advance with great power throughout the earth until there is a millennial kingdom on the earth.

According to this view, Jesus will return at the end of this millennial age. Then there will be one resurrection of both believers and unbelievers. Those who believe in him will go to heaven; those who don't will face the final judgment and eternal condemnation. At that time the new heavens and new earth will begin and remain for eternity, and Christ will be present on earth to reign in bodily form. This view is called the *post*millennial view because Christ's return and reign will occur *after* a future millennium.

View 3—Premillennial: The millennium will come suddenly, and Jesus will return before the millennium

Finally, there are Christians who believe Jesus will return *before* the events of Revelation 20:1–10. This is called the premillennial view because it holds that Christ will return before the millennium. This view also holds that prior to Jesus' return there will be a time of great suffering on the earth, sometimes called the great tribulation (see Matt. 24:21–31).

According to the premillennial view, Christ will return and physically reign on earth for the thousand years mentioned in Revelation 20:4–5 (not necessarily a literal one thousand years). When Christ returns to begin his millennial reign, all who have believed in him will be raised from the dead to reign with him. This is the meaning of Revelation 20:4, "They came to life and reigned with Christ for a thousand years."

During that millennium, Satan and his demons will be completely removed from all influence on the earth, as described in Revelation 20:1–3:

Then I saw an angel coming down from heaven, holding in his hand the key to the bottomless pit and a great chain. And he seized the dragon, that ancient serpent, who is the devil and Satan, and bound him for a thousand years, and threw him into the pit, and shut it and sealed it over him,

so that he might not deceive the nations any longer, until the
thousand years were ended. After that he must be released
for a little while.

Because Jesus will reign in peace and righteousness over
the earth, many people on the earth will turn to him for their
salvation. But there will still be unbelievers on the earth just
as there were some who "doubted" after they had seen Jesus
in his resurrected body (Matt. 28:17). Some will not believe
because genuine faith is something that must come from an
internally changed heart and cannot be compelled even by
overwhelming outward evidence and arguments. Even with
no influence from Satan or demons at all on the earth, there
will still be people who do evil, showing that our sin is not
really caused by Satan but is the responsibility of the human
beings who do the sin.

In this premillennial view, after the thousand-year reign of
Christ on the earth, the final judgment will occur, and those
who believe in Jesus will continue to reign with him for eternity; those who rejected him will be condemned for eternity.

The Bible seems to support this position more than the
others. It is an easy and natural reading of Revelation 20:1–6,
and many have understood it in this way since the early
church. In addition, Old Testament passages such as Isaiah
65:20 indicate a time in the future that is very different from
this age yet when sin and death are not removed: "No more
shall there be in it an infant who lives but a few days, or an old
man who does not fill out his days, for the young man shall
die a hundred years old, and the sinner a hundred years old
shall be accursed." Other passages, such as Psalm 72:8–14;
Isaiah 11:2–9; Zechariah 14:6–21; 1 Corinthians 15:24; and
Revelation 2:27; 12:5; and 19:15, seem to indicate a period of

time when Christ's reign over all things is seen in a greater way but sin and evil still exist on the earth. This fits a picture of Christ's future millennial reign.

In addition, a future but not final reign of Christ is supported by passages such as Revelation 2:26–27, which indicate a ruling with "a rod of iron" over a rebellious people. This type of rule is indicative of a premillennial reign of Christ. This reign seems to be well supported by other New Testament passages that affirm that believers in Jesus will reign over the earth with him sometime in the future (Luke 19:17, 19; 1 Cor. 6:3; Rev. 2:26–27; 3:21).

One variation on the premillennial view has had many followers in the United States. Since it holds that Christ will come back before the great "tribulation" mentioned in Matthew 24:21–31, this view is called a *pretribulational* premillennial view. Those who hold this view believe that Christ will actually return twice: once in a secret return to suddenly take Christians out of the world and then seven years later in a second, public return when he will bring Christians back to earth to reign with him for the thousand years mentioned in Revelation 20:4–5. During the seven years when Christ and Christians are absent from the earth, there will be a time of great tribulation when the vast majority of Jewish people will trust in Christ as their Messiah and preach the gospel to those left on earth.

The difficulty with this position is that it is hard to find any passages that speak about a secret return of Christ. The passages that speak of Christ's return always speak of it in very visible, public terms, such as 1 Thessalonians 4:16: "For the Lord himself will descend from heaven with a cry of command, with the voice of an archangel, and with the sound of the trumpet of God."

The Victorious King

It is perhaps not surprising that Christians have differences over their views of the future. This is due in part to the subject matter: the future is somewhat unclear to us since it has not yet happened! But regardless of the timing of Christ's return, all Christians believe that the final victory of Christ over Satan (described in Revelation 20:7–10) will occur in the future. They believe that Satan "will be released from his prison" (Rev. 20:7) to gather together for battle those he has deceived. At that final battle, Jesus will defeat Satan and his army once and for all. At the end of the battle, Satan will be "thrown into the lake of fire and sulfur" where he "will be tormented day and night forever and ever" (Rev. 20:10). At the end of the final battle, Jesus, the victorious King, will execute his final judgment. And then he will reign forever and ever.

As Jesus told John, this is something in which Christians can take great hope, because his words "are trustworthy and true" (Rev. 22:6). Jesus said, "I am coming soon, bringing my recompense with me, to repay each one for what he has done" (Rev. 22:12). The response of those who are believers in Jesus, regardless of their interpretation of Revelation 20:1–6, should be like John's: "Amen. Come, Lord Jesus!" (Rev. 22:20).

Questions for Review and Application

1. What are some of the things about eschatology that all Christians should agree on? Which of those things gives you the greatest joy?

2. What are some issues relating to eschatology that Christians differ on? How should Christians deal with these differences?

3. Take a moment to read Revelation 22:12. In response to reading that, take a moment to pray John's prayer as found in Revelation 22:20.

chapter

WHAT IS THE FINAL JUDGMENT?

A fter the thousand-year reign of Christ (according to any of the views discussed in the last chapter) and after the final defeat of Satan and his army, Jesus Christ will judge all people from his "great white throne" (Rev. 20:11–15).

This final judgment is the culmination of many precursors throughout history in which God rewarded righteousness or punished unrighteousness (for example, the flood in Genesis 6–8 or the fiery destruction of Sodom and Gomorrah in Genesis 19:1–26). The final judgment is the "day of wrath when God's righteous judgment will be revealed" (Rom. 2:5). It is the day God has determined when "he will judge the world in righteousness" through Christ (Acts 17:31).

What Happens at the Final Judgment?

Jesus "is the one appointed by God to be judge of the living and the dead" (Acts 10:42; see also Matt. 25:31–33; 2 Tim. 4:1). His "authority to execute judgment" was given to him by God (John 5:27). This "time for the dead to be judged" will be a time for "rewarding" God's servants and a time for "destroying the destroyers of the earth" (Rev. 11:18). Therefore, at this time, both those who believe in Jesus and those who do not believe in him will be judged.

As for unbelievers, Paul says, "For those who are self-seeking and do not obey the truth, but obey unrighteousness, there will be wrath and fury" (Rom. 2:8). Already in the Old Testament there was an assurance that "God will bring every deed into judgment, with every secret thing, whether good or evil" (Eccl. 12:14). Those who haven't looked to Jesus for their salvation will be judged according to what they have done (Rev. 20:12). God will be fair. The degree of punishment will vary according to what each person has done, for some "will receive the greater condemnation" (Luke 20:47). According to Jesus' teaching on the difference between the servant who knew his master's will and the one who did not (Luke 12:47–48), it seems that punishment will also vary according to how much knowledge people had of God's requirements.

We who believe in Jesus will also "stand before the judgment seat of God" to "give an account" of ourselves to God (Rom. 14:10–12). But the final judgment for believers will not be one of punishment, but one of reward. Jesus promises in John 5:24, "Whoever hears my word and believes him who sent me has eternal life. *He does not come into judgment,* but has passed from death to life." Paul confirms this when he writes in Romans 8:1, "There is . . . no condemnation for those who are in Christ Jesus."

Therefore, the final judgment should not be a source of fear for believers but instead an encouragement for them to make it their aim "to please" God (2 Cor. 5:9). Every sin we have committed has been eternally paid for by Christ and therefore eternally forgiven by God. At the judgment, we will receive rewards due us for what we have "done in the body, whether good or evil" (2 Cor. 5:10). The evil will pass away, and the good will be rewarded (1 Cor. 3:12–15).

Although there will be degrees of reward in heaven, everyone's joy will be complete. This is because our joy will not come from what we possess or our status but from our relationship with God. In heaven, our joy in fully delighting in God, our joy in being able to be in his presence and fall down before his throne to worship him, will be greater than the joy found in any reward (Rev. 4:10–11).

Instead of fostering a spirit of competition, the fact that we will receive a reward for what we have done should spur us on to "consider how to stir up one another to love and good works, not neglecting to meet together, as is the habit of some, but encouraging one another" all the more as the final judgment appears to be drawing near (Heb. 10:24–25).

Believers and unbelievers are not the only ones who will be judged. Jude 6 and 2 Peter 2:4 tell us that the rebellious angels will also be judged, and 1 Corinthians 6:3 indicates that the good angels will be evaluated for their work and service.

The Purpose of the Final Judgment

The final judgment will not take place so that God can determine the condition of each person's heart, for he has known the final condition of every heart before time began. Instead, the final judgment will take place so that God can display his glory to all mankind by demonstrating his justice and mercy simultaneously.

The final judgment will be entirely fair. Each person, whether destined for eternal glory or eternal condemnation, will be dealt with more fairly at the final judgment than at any previous time. God will judge "impartially according to each one's deeds" (1 Peter 1:17), "for God shows no partiality" (Rom. 2:11). God will be so glorified in his final judgment that we will cry, "Hallelujah! Salvation and glory and power belong to our God, for his judgments are true and just" (Rev. 19:1–2).

The Application of the Final Judgment

Because there is a final judgment, we are assured that God's universe is fair. It satisfies our inward sense of a need for justice in the world. The final judgment assures us that regardless of what happens, God is in control and will eventually bring about a right end to every situation. Paul writes in Colossians 3:25, "The wrongdoer will be paid back for the wrong he has done, and there is no partiality."

Therefore, in light of the final judgment, Christians should be able to forgive each other freely, for we know that all accounts will be settled on that day and all wrongs will be made right. Because there is a final judgment, Christians should never seek to avenge themselves but instead "leave it to the wrath of God, for it is written, 'Vengeance is mine, I will repay, says the Lord'" (Rom. 12:19). When we are wronged, we can take the desire for justice to God, asking that he work out justice on our behalf. We can be confident that the punishment due the offender will be executed; it will either fall on the shoulders of Christ or on the shoulders of the offender for all eternity. When we act in this way, we are following the example of Christ, for "when he was reviled, he did not revile in return; when he suffered, he did not threaten, but continued entrusting himself to him who judges justly" (1 Peter 2:23).

The final judgment also provides us with motivation to live each day in obedience to God and thus to "lay up . . . treasures in heaven" (Matt. 6:20). Even though these treasures do not earn us our salvation, they do reward us for the good we have done.

The final judgment also provides us with an encouragement to tell others about the good news of Jesus. The delay of the Lord's return and final judgment is because God does not wish "that any should perish, but that all should reach repentance" (2 Peter 3:9). Therefore, those who believe in Jesus should share the good news of what they believe with others. The Bible's clear warnings of final judgment should encourage unbelievers to turn from their sin and to look to Jesus for their salvation.

What about Hell?

At the final judgment, those who have rejected the claims of Jesus will go to a place of eternal punishment. That place of eternal punishment, the Bible tells us, is hell.

The Bible's descriptions of hell are difficult to read, and they should be deeply disturbing to us. Jesus speaks of hell as "the eternal fire prepared for the devil and his angels," and he says that those who have rejected him will also go there (Matt. 25:41). It is a place where the "worm does not die and the fire is not quenched" (Mark 9:48). It is a "place of torment" (Luke 16:28). John tells us it is a place where those who rejected Jesus will, along with the devil and his angels, "drink the wine of God's wrath, poured full strength into the cup of his anger" and "be tormented with fire and sulfur in the presence of the holy angels and in the presence of the Lamb" (Rev. 14:10). The "smoke of their torment" will go on "forever and ever, and they have no rest, day or night" (Rev. 14:11).

While we who have believed in Christ should have no fear of hell, we should still think of it only with great solemnity and sadness. Even God himself says, "I have no pleasure in the death of the wicked" (Ezek. 33:11). Although it is hard to think about, the doctrine of hell is so clearly taught in Scripture that there does not seem to be any acceptable way to deny it and still be subject to God's Word. In addition, in a universe where there is deep and profound evil that calls forth the just wrath of a righteous, holy God, we should also realize that evil cannot simply go unpunished. All of God's judgments are just and right, because "the LORD is upright . . . there is no unrighteousness in him" (Ps. 92:15).

Questions for Review and Application

1. What happens to Christians at the final judgment? What will happen to those who have rejected Jesus' claims?
2. How does your understanding of the final judgment affect your life today? How does it affect the way you relate to others?
3. What does the Bible tell us about hell? How does your understanding of hell make you feel? Why does it make you feel that way?

chapter 20

WHAT IS HEAVEN?

After the final judgment, those who believe in Jesus will enter into the full enjoyment of life that they have longed for.

They will hear Jesus say something like "Come, you who are blessed by my Father, inherit the kingdom prepared for you from the foundation of the world" (Matt. 25:34), and they will live for eternity in the presence of God. While people often refer to this kingdom as simply "heaven," the Bible actually paints an even richer picture of a new heaven and new earth.

The Bible promises an entirely renewed creation. It will be "the new heavens and the new earth" that God will make (Isa. 66:22), a place so rich and good and new that "the former things"—like death, pain, sorrow, and suffering—"shall not be remembered or come to mind" (Isa. 65:17). It is a place where heaven and earth will join together (Rev. 21:2), and a voice from God's throne will announce, "Behold, the dwelling place of God is with man. He will dwell with them, and they will be his people, and God himself will be with them as their God" (Rev. 21:3).

The Renewed Heaven and Earth

The Bible frequently refers to the place God currently dwells as "heaven." For example, Jesus taught his disciples to pray,

"Our Father in heaven" (Matt. 6:9). Peter says Jesus "has gone into heaven and is at the right hand of God" (1 Peter 3:22). Heaven is the place where God most fully makes known his presence to bless. Although God is everywhere, his presence to bless is most clearly seen in heaven, and his glory is most clearly seen in heaven. Heaven is the one place where everyone worships him.

In addition to making a renewed heaven, God will renew his earthly creation—the earth and those who will dwell in it (2 Peter 3:13; Rev. 21:1). Paul writes in Romans 8:21, "The creation itself will be set free from its bondage to corruption and obtain the freedom of the glory of the children of God." No longer will there be the "thorns and thistles" (Gen. 3:18) that God brought in judgment on sin, nor will there be other distortions of nature that bring destruction, such as hurricanes and tornadoes, floods, droughts, and earthquakes. Paradise will be restored.

Those who live on the renewed earth will have new, glorified bodies that will never grow old or become weak or ill. With the curse of sin removed, all creation will be returned to its original state, which was "very good" (Gen. 1:31).

Life in the renewed heavens and earth will include many of the good things about life here on earth, only they will all be much better: all will eat and drink at the marriage supper of the Lamb (Rev. 19:9); Jesus will once again drink wine with his disciples (Luke 22:18); the "river of the water of life" will flow "through the middle of the street of the city"; and the "tree of life" will yield twelve kinds of fruit—one for each month (Rev. 22:1–3).

Music is certainly prominent in the descriptions of heaven in Revelation. It appears that music and other artistic activities will be done with all excellence to the glory of God. Humans will probably continue to exercise dominion over the earth and its resources through technological, creative, and inventive means, fully reflecting their creation in the image of God. And although human beings in their new bodies will be like God, they won't be God. So, for example, we will not have infinite knowledge but will forever continue to increase in the knowledge of God, who alone is infinite (Col. 1:10).

Finally, the renewed heavens and earth will be a place where we can fully enjoy the "treasures in heaven" (Matt. 6:20) that we have been storing up for ourselves during our life on earth. This is wonderful encouragement for us to "do good to everyone, and especially to those who are of the household of faith" (Gal. 6:10). Therefore, as believers in Jesus, we ought to live "lives of holiness and godliness" while we are "waiting for new heavens and a new earth in which righteousness dwells" (2 Peter 3:11, 13).

The Undeniable Glory of God

In addition to being a place of unimaginable beauty, heaven will be a place where God's glory is so undeniably evident that all of creation will function in a way that is in full cooperation with his will. Therefore, the world will no longer be "broken"; it will work like it is supposed to. And all the people there will also no longer be "broken," for they will work and act and relate to one another like they are supposed to. There will no longer be any pain or sorrow, grief or tragedy, for God himself will dwell with his people. "He will wipe away every tear from their eyes, and death shall be no more, neither shall there be mourning, nor crying, nor pain anymore, for the former things have passed away" (Rev. 21:4).

But even more exciting is the fact that God's fellowship

with us will be unhindered. We will forever be able to interact with him and worship him as we were designed to do. The city will have no need of light, "for the glory of God gives it light, and its lamp is the Lamb" (Rev. 21:23). This will be the fulfillment of God's purpose to call us "to his own glory and excellence" (2 Peter 1:3). We will forever dwell in "the presence of his glory with great joy" (Jude 24; see also Rom. 8:18; 1 Cor. 15:43; 2 Cor. 4:17; 1 Thess. 2:12; 1 Peter 5:4, 10).

Our greatest joy will be that we "will see his face" (Rev. 22:4). The sight of God's face will be the fulfillment of everything we know to be good, right, and desirable in the universe. In God's face, we will see and experience the fulfillment of all the longing we have ever had—the longing to know perfect love, peace, and joy, to know truth and justice, holiness and wisdom, goodness and power, glory and beauty. We will discover that in God's presence "there is fullness of joy" and at his right hand "pleasures forevermore" (Ps. 16:11).

Questions for Review and Application

1. Can you list some of the things the Bible says about heaven?
2. In what ways does the Bible's description of heaven surprise you, encourage you, and make you long for heaven even more?
3. Take a moment to pray, thanking God for specific aspects of heaven.

appendix 1

HISTORIC CONFESSIONS OF FAITH

This appendix reprints three of the most significant confessions of faith from the ancient church: the Apostles' Creed (third–fourth centuries AD), the Nicene Creed (AD 325/381), and the Chalcedonian Creed (AD 451). I have also included the Chicago Statement on Biblical Inerrancy (1978) because it was the product of a conference representing a broad variety of evangelical traditions and because it has gained widespread acceptance as a valuable doctrinal standard concerning an issue of recent and current controversy in the church.

The Apostles' Creed
(Third–fourth centuries AD)

I believe in God the Father Almighty; Maker of heaven and earth.

And in Jesus Christ his only Son our Lord; who was conceived by the Holy Spirit,[1] born of the virgin Mary; suffered

---

1. I have used the modern translation "Holy Spirit" instead of the archaic name "Holy Ghost" throughout the ancient creeds.

under Pontius Pilate, was crucified, dead and buried;[2] the third day he rose from the dead; he ascended into heaven; and sitteth at the right hand of God the Father Almighty; from thence he shall come to judge the quick and the dead.

I believe in the Holy Spirit; the holy catholic Church; the communion of saints; the forgiveness of sins; the resurrection of the body; and the life everlasting. Amen.

The Nicene Creed
(AD 325; revised at Constantinople AD 381)

I believe in one God the Father Almighty; Maker of heaven and earth, and of all things visible and invisible.

And in one Lord Jesus Christ, the only-begotten Son of God, begotten of the Father before all worlds, God of Gods, Light of Light, very God of very God, begotten, not made, being of one substance with the Father; by whom all things were made; who, for us men and for our salvation, came down from heaven, and was incarnate by the Holy Spirit of the Virgin Mary, and was made man; and was crucified also for us under Pontius Pilate; he suffered and was buried; and the third day he rose again, according to the Scriptures; and ascended into heaven, and sitteth on the right hand of the Father; and he shall come again, with glory, to judge both the quick and the dead; whose kingdom shall have no end.

And in the Holy Spirit, the Lord and Giver of Life; who proceedeth from the Father and the Son;[3] who with the Father

---

2. I have not included the phrase "he descended into hell" because it is not attested in the earliest versions of the Apostles' Creed and because of the doctrinal difficulties associated with it.

3. The phrase "and the Son" was added after the Council of Constantinople in 381 but is commonly included in the text of the Nicene Creed as used by Protestant

and the Son together is worshiped and glorified; who spake by the Prophets. And one Holy Catholic and Apostolic Church. I acknowledge one Baptism for the remission of sins; and I look for the resurrection of the dead, and the life of the world to come. Amen.

The Chalcedonian Creed
(AD 451)

We, then, following the holy Fathers, all with one consent, teach men to confess one and the same Son, our Lord Jesus Christ, the same perfect in Godhead and also perfect in manhood; truly God and truly man, of a reasonable soul and body; consubstantial with the Father according to the Godhead, and consubstantial with us according to the Manhood; in all things like unto us, without sin; begotten before all ages of the Father according to the Godhead, and in these latter days, for us and for our salvation, born of the Virgin Mary, the Mother of God, according to the Manhood; one and the same Christ, Son, Lord, Only-begotten, to be acknowledged in two natures, inconfusedly, unchangeably, indivisibly, inseparably; the distinction of natures being by no means taken away by the union, but rather the property of each nature being preserved, and concurring in one Person and one Subsistence, not parted or divided into two persons, but one and the same Son, and only begotten, God the Word, the Lord Jesus Christ, as the prophets from the beginning have declared concerning him, and the Lord Jesus Christ himself has taught us, and the Creed of the holy Fathers has handed down to us.

---

and Roman Catholic churches today. The phrase is not included in the text used by Orthodox churches.

The Chicago Statement on Biblical Inerrancy
(1978)

Preface

The authority of Scripture is a key issue for the Christian Church in this and every age. Those who profess faith in Jesus Christ as Lord and Savior are called to show the reality of their discipleship by humbly and faithfully obeying God's written Word. To stray from Scripture in faith or conduct is disloyalty to our Master. Recognition of the total truth and trustworthiness of Holy Scripture is essential to a full grasp and adequate confession of its authority.

The following Statement affirms this inerrancy of Scripture afresh, making clear our understanding of it and warning against its denial. We are persuaded that to deny it is to set aside the witness of Jesus Christ and of the Holy Spirit and to refuse that submission to the claims of God's own Word which marks true Christian faith. We see it as our timely duty to make this affirmation in the face of current lapses from the truth of inerrancy among our fellow Christians and misunderstanding of this doctrine in the world at large.

This Statement consists of three parts: a Summary Statement, Articles of Affirmation and Denial, and an accompanying Exposition [not included in this appendix]. It has been prepared in the course of a three-day consultation in Chicago. Those who have signed the Summary Statement and the Articles wish to affirm their own conviction as to the inerrancy of Scripture and to encourage and challenge one another and all Christians to growing appreciation and understanding of this doctrine. We acknowledge the limitations of a document prepared in a brief, intensive conference and do not propose that this Statement be given creedal weight. Yet we rejoice in the deepening of our own convictions through our discussions together, and we pray that the Statement we have signed may be used to the glory of our God toward a new reformation of the Church in its faith, life, and mission.

We offer this Statement in a spirit, not of contention, but of humility and love, which we purpose by God's grace to maintain in any future dialogue arising out of what we have said. We gladly acknowledge that many who deny the inerrancy of Scripture do not display the consequences of this denial in the rest of their belief and behavior, and we are conscious that we who confess this doctrine often deny it in life by failing to bring our thoughts and deeds, our traditions and habits, into true subjection to the divine Word.

We invite responses to this statement from any who see reason to amend its affirmations about Scripture by the light of Scripture itself, under whose infallible authority we stand as we speak. We claim no personal infallibility for the witness we bear, and for any help which enables us to strengthen this testimony to God's Word we shall be grateful.

Summary Statement

1. God, who is Himself Truth and speaks truth only, has inspired Holy Scripture in order thereby to reveal Himself to lost mankind through Jesus Christ as Creator and Lord, Redeemer and Judge. Holy Scripture is God's witness to Himself.

2. Holy Scripture, being God's own Word, written by men prepared and superintended by His Spirit, is of infallible divine authority in all matters upon which it touches: it is to be believed, as God's instruction, in all that it affirms; obeyed, as God's command, in all that it requires; embraced, as God's pledge, in all that it promises.

3. The Holy Spirit, Scripture's divine Author, both authenticates it to us by His inward witness and opens our minds to understand its meaning.

4. Being wholly and verbally God-given, Scripture is without error or fault in all its teaching, no less in what it states about God's acts in creation, about the events of world history, and about its own literary origins under God, than in its witness to God's saving grace in individual lives.

5. The authority of Scripture is inescapably impaired if this total divine inerrancy is in any way limited or disregarded, or made relative to a view of truth contrary to the Bible's own; and such lapses bring serious loss to both the individual and the Church.

Articles of Affirmation and Denial

Article I

We affirm that the Holy Scriptures are to be received as the authoritative Word of God.

We deny that the Scriptures receive their authority from the Church, tradition, or any other human source.

Article II

We affirm that the Scriptures are the supreme written norm by which God binds the conscience, and that the authority of the Church is subordinate to that of Scripture.

We deny that Church creeds, councils, or declarations have authority greater than or equal to the authority of the Bible.

Article III

We affirm that the written Word in its entirety is revelation given by God.

We deny that the Bible is merely a witness to revelation,

or only becomes revelation in encounter, or depends on the responses of men for its validity.

Article IV

We affirm that God who made mankind in His image has used language as a means of revelation.

We deny that human language is so limited by our creatureliness that it is rendered inadequate as a vehicle for divine revelation. We further deny that the corruption of human culture and language through sin has thwarted God's work of inspiration.

Article V

We affirm that God's revelation in the Holy Scriptures was progressive. We deny that later revelation, which may fulfill earlier revelation, ever corrects or contradicts it. We further deny that any normative revelation has been given since the completion of the New Testament writings.

Article VI

We affirm that the whole of Scripture and all its parts, down to the very words of the original, were given by divine inspiration.

We deny that the inspiration of Scripture can rightly be affirmed of the whole without the parts, or of some parts but not the whole.

Article VII

We affirm that inspiration was the work in which God by His Spirit, through human writers, gave us His Word. The origin of Scripture is divine. The mode of divine inspiration remains largely a mystery to us.

We deny that inspiration can be reduced to human insight, or to heightened states of consciousness of any kind.

Article VIII

We affirm that God in His Work of inspiration utilized the distinctive personalities and literary styles of the writers whom He had chosen and prepared.

We deny that God, in causing these writers to use the very words that He chose, overrode their personalities.

Article IX

We affirm that inspiration, though not conferring omniscience, guaranteed true and trustworthy utterance on all matters of which the Bible authors were moved to speak and write.

We deny that the finitude or fallenness of these writers, by necessity or otherwise, introduced distortion or falsehood into God's Word.

Article X

We affirm that inspiration, strictly speaking, applies to the autographic text of Scripture, which in the providence of God can be ascertained from available manuscripts with great accuracy. We further affirm that copies and translations of Scripture are the Word of God to the extent that they faithfully represent the original.

We deny that any essential element of the Christian faith is affected by the absence of the autographs. We further deny that this absence renders the assertion of Biblical inerrancy invalid or irrelevant.

Article XI

We affirm that Scripture, having been given by divine

inspiration, is infallible, so that, far from misleading us, it is true and reliable in all matters it addresses.

We deny that it is possible for the Bible to be at the same time infallible and errant in its assertions. Infallibility and inerrancy may be distinguished, but not separated.

Article XII

We affirm that Scripture in its entirety is inerrant, being free from all falsehood, fraud, or deceit.

We deny that Biblical infallibility and inerrancy are limited to spiritual, religious or redemptive themes, exclusive of assertions in the fields of history and science. We further deny that scientific hypotheses about earth history may properly be used to overturn the teaching of Scripture on creation and the flood.

Article XIII

We affirm the propriety of using inerrancy as a theological term with reference to the complete truthfulness of Scripture.

We deny that it is proper to evaluate Scripture according to standards of truth and error that are alien to its usage or purpose. We further deny that inerrancy is negated by Biblical phenomena such as a lack of modern technical precision, irregularities of grammar or spelling, observational descriptions of nature, the reporting of falsehoods, the use of hyperbole and round numbers, the topical arrangement of material, variant selections of material in parallel accounts, or the use of free citations.

Article XIV

We affirm the unity and internal consistency of Scripture.

We deny that alleged errors and discrepancies that have not yet been resolved vitiate the truth of claims of the Bible.

Article XV

We affirm that the doctrine of inerrancy is grounded in the teaching of the Bible about inspiration.

We deny that Jesus' teaching about Scripture may be dismissed by appeals to accommodation or to any natural limitation of His humanity.

Article XVI

We affirm that the doctrine of inerrancy has been integral to the Church's faith throughout its history.

We deny that inerrancy is a doctrine invented by Scholastic Protestantism, or is a reactionary position postulated in response to negative higher criticism.

Article XVII

We affirm that the Holy Spirit bears witness to the Scriptures, assuring believers of the truthfulness of God's written Word.

We deny that this witness of the Holy Spirit operates in isolation from or against Scripture.

Article XVIII

We affirm that the text of Scripture is to be interpreted by grammatico-historical exegesis, taking account of its literary forms and devices, and that Scripture is to interpret Scripture.

We deny the legitimacy of any treatment of the text or quest for sources lying behind it that leads to relativizing, dehistoricizing, or discounting its teaching, or rejecting its claims to authorship.

Article XIX

We affirm that a confession of the full authority, infallibility, and inerrancy of Scripture is vital to a sound understanding of the whole of the Christian faith. We further affirm that such confession should lead to increasing conformity to the image of Christ.

We deny that such confession is necessary for salvation. However, we further deny that inerrancy can be rejected without grave consequences, both to the individual and to the Church.

appendix **2**

BOOKS FOR FURTHER READING IN SYSTEMATIC THEOLOGY

Some readers may wish to do more study in the topics covered in this book. The general field for such study of Christian beliefs is called "systematic theology." For more detailed treatment of the topics in this book and many other topics, I suggest that readers begin with one of two longer books I have written on these subjects:

> Wayne Grudem. *Systematic Theology: An Introduction to Biblical Doctrine.* 2nd ed. Grand Rapids: Zondervan; London, UK: Inter-Varsity Press, 2020 (1,586 pages).
> Wayne Grudem. *Bible Doctrine: Essential Teachings of the Christian Faith.* 2nd ed. Edited by Alexander Grudem. Grand Rapids: Zondervan; London, UK: Inter-Varsity Press, 2022 (672 pages): a condensed version of *Systematic Theology*).

In addition to these works, the following bibliography lists some other evangelical systematic theologies available in English and also a few shorter guides to Christian doctrine.

I have indicated the broad theological tradition for each author, and I have sought to include one or two volumes from each of the main theological and denominational traditions within the evangelical world.

With the exception of the two Roman Catholic books, which I included to give some access to Roman Catholicism (the traditional theology text by Ott, and the 1994 *Catechism of the Catholic Church*), all of the authors on this list fall generally within a "conservative evangelical" theological position.[1]

Allen, Michael, and Scott R. Swain. *Christian Dogmatics: Reformed Theology for the Church Catholic.* Grand Rapids, Baker: 2016.

A compilation of sixteen essays on major Christian doctrines, written by twelve contemporary Reformed scholars.

Allison, Gregg R. *50 Core Truths of the Christian Faith: A Guide to Understanding and Teaching Theology.* Grand Rapids: Baker, 2018.

————. *Historical Theology: An Introduction to Christian Doctrine; A Companion to Wayne Grudem's* Systematic Theology. Grand Rapids: Zondervan, 2011.

Allison is professor of Christian theology at the Southern Baptist Theological Seminary in Louisville, Kentucky.

---

1. A very helpful and more broadly based annotated bibliography, including notes on works from several prominent liberal scholars, may be found in John Jefferson Davis, *Theology Primer* (Grand Rapids: Baker, 1981), 74–79; see also his "Brief Guide to Modern Theologians" on pp. 39–55. In addition, valuable brief notes on dozens of important theologians from all theological traditions may be found in Millard Erickson, *Concise Dictionary of Christian Theology* (Grand Rapids: Baker, 1986). See also Stanley J. Grenz and Roger E. Olson, *20th Century Theology* (Downers Grove, IL: InterVarsity Press, 1992).

Bavinck, Herman. *Reformed Dogmatics*. Edited by John Bolt. Translated by John Vriend. 4 vols. Grand Rapids: Baker, 2008.

Bavinck (1854–1921) was a Dutch theologian and one of the most brilliant spokesmen for a Reformed theological position.

Berkhof, Louis. *Systematic Theology*. 4th ed. Grand Rapids: Eerdmans, 1939.

In 1996 this book was reissued with Berkhof's *Introduction to Systematic Theology* bound with it in one volume. This is the standard Reformed textbook for systematic theology, written by a former president of Calvin Seminary in Grand Rapids, Michigan. The book is a great treasure house of information and analysis, and it is probably the most useful one-volume systematic theology available from any theological perspective. Berkhof lived from 1873 to 1957.

Bird, Michael F. *Evangelical Theology: A Biblical and Systematic Introduction*. 2nd ed. Grand Rapids: Zondervan, 2020.

A very readable systematic theology structured around the message of the gospel, written by a New Testament scholar who is academic dean at Ridley College in Melbourne, Australia.

Boice, James Montgomery. *Foundations of the Christian Faith*. Rev. one-vol. ed. Downers Grove, IL: InterVarsity Press, 1986.

This Reformed guide to systematic theology was written by the late theologian-pastor of Tenth Presbyterian Church in

Philadelphia. The book is written in a popular, readable style with helpful application of doctrines to life. It was previously published in four separate volumes: *The Sovereign God* (1978), *God the Redeemer* (1978), *Awakening to God* (1979), and *God and History* (1981). Boice lived from 1938 to 2000.

Boyce, James Pettigru. *Abstract of Systematic Theology*. 1887. Reprint, n.p.: Christian Gospel Foundation, n.d.

This Baptist systematic theology is also Reformed in doctrinal orientation. Boyce (1827–88) was the president of the Southern Baptist Seminary in Louisville, Kentucky, and a professor of systematic theology there.

Bray, Gerald. *God Has Spoken: A History of Christian Theology*. Wheaton, IL: Crossway, 2014.

Bray is a remarkably erudite Anglican scholar who says his aim in this book is "to make the history of Christian theology comprehensible to nonspecialists while at the same time providing a useful resource for those who want to take the subject further" (p. 22). Bray is now retired, but he taught for many years at Beeson Divinity School in Birmingham, Alabama.

Calvin, John. *Institutes of the Christian Religion*. Edited by John T. McNeill. Translated and indexed by Ford Lewis Battles. The Library of Christian Classics, vols. 20–21. Philadelphia: Westminster, 1960. Translated from the 1559 text and collated with earlier versions.

This is the best available English translation of Calvin's systematic exposition of the Christian faith. Calvin (1509–64) was a French reformer who became the greatest theologian of the Reformation and, according to many estimates, the greatest theologian in the history of the church. The book is Reformed in doctrinal perspective.

Carter, Charles W., ed. *A Contemporary Wesleyan Theology: Biblical, Systematic, and Practical.* 2 vols. Grand Rapids: Francis Asbury Press, an imprint of Zondervan, 1983.

This is a collection of twenty-four essays on major doctrinal themes by several scholars representing a wide range of conservative Wesleyan denominations and institutions. The set also includes some essays on practical theology and ethics. Charles Carter, who contributed four of the chapters, was professor of religion and missions at Marion College (now Indiana Wesleyan University) in Marion, Indiana. The advisory committee for the volumes included representatives of the United Methodist Church, Free Methodist Church, Church of the Nazarene, Missionary Church, Salvation Army, Wesleyan Church, and others.

Catechism of the Catholic Church. English translation. San Francisco: Ignatius Press, 1994.

This is the best current statement of the doctrinal positions of the Roman Catholic Church. It was prepared by a commission of cardinals and bishops under the direction of Cardinal Joseph Ratzinger (now Pope Benedict XVI). Upon its publication, Pope John Paul II wrote that it "is a statement of the Church's faith and of catholic doctrine. . . . I declare it to be a sure norm for teaching the faith. . . . This catechism is given . . . that it may be a sure and authentic reference text for teaching catholic doctrine" (p. 5).

Chafer, Lewis Sperry. *Systematic Theology*. 7 vols. plus index
vol. Dallas: Dallas Seminary Press, 1947–48.
————. *Systematic Theology: Abridged Edition*. 2 vols. Edited
by John F. Walvoord, Donald K. Campbell, and Roy B.
Zuck. Wheaton, IL: Victor Books, 1988.

Chafer (1871–1952) was the first president of Dallas
Theological Seminary. The seven-volume edition is the most
extensive dispensational systematic theology ever written. The
two-volume edition is a condensation of the earlier work.

Cottrell, Jack. *The Faith Once for All: Bible Doctrine for
Today*. Joplin, MO: College Press, 2002.

Cottrell is an articulate and thoughtful Arminian theologian who taught at Cincinnati Bible Seminary (Christian
Church/Churches of Christ).

Duffield, Guy P., and Nathaniel M. Van Cleave. *Foundations of
Pentecostal Theology*. Lake Mary, FL: Creation House, 2008.

An extensive treatment of Christian doctrine, written by
two veteran Pentecostal pastor-teachers, with extensive discussion of "baptism with the Holy Spirit," various spiritual gifts,
and much material on divine healing.

Edwards, Jonathan. *The Works of Jonathan Edwards*. 2 vols.
Revised and corrected by Edward Hickman. 1834.
Reprint, Edinburgh: Banner of Truth, 1974.

Edwards (1703–58) was a pastor in Northampton, Massa-
chusetts, and for one month before his death from a smallpox

injection, president of Princeton. Some consider him the greatest American philosopher-theologian. He did not write an entire systematic theology, but his works contain writings on most theological topics. He was strongly Reformed in outlook and combined profound thought with warm-hearted devotion to Christ. (A new edition of Edwards's works is in process of publication from Yale University Press.)

> Erickson, Millard. *Christian Theology*. 3rd ed. Grand Rapids: Baker, 2013.

This is a clear and very thorough textbook in systematic theology from a Baptist perspective. Erickson was academic dean at Bethel Theological Seminary in St. Paul, Minnesota. This book includes interaction with all the major trends in contemporary nonevangelical theology as well as helpful material for personal application. Erickson has also published a condensed version of this book, *Introducing Christian Doctrine*, edited by L. Arnold Hustad (Grand Rapids: Baker, 1992).

> Frame, John. *Systematic Theology: An Introduction to Christian Belief*. Phillipsburg, NJ: P&R, 2013.

This excellent volume is a wonderfully clear, refreshingly insightful, and profoundly biblical treatment of systematic theology, written by a now-retired professor of systematic theology at Reformed Theological Seminary in Orlando, Florida, who previously had taught at Westminster Seminary California and Westminster Theological Seminary in Philadelphia.

> Garrett, James Leo. *Systematic Theology: Biblical, Historical, Evangelical*. 2 vols. Grand Rapids: Eerdmans, 1990, 1995.

Garrett (1925–2020), a Southern Baptist, was Distinguished Professor of Theology at Southwestern Baptist Theological Seminary in Fort Worth, Texas. He interacts extensively and with scrupulous fairness with both evangelical and nonevangelical authors, though he himself is firmly within the evangelical camp. He is Baptistic in his convictions yet gives much more space to representing different positions clearly than to arguing for his own position. With 1,530 total pages, these volumes are an amazingly rich resource for historical, bibliographical, and biblical data on each doctrine treated.

Geisler, Norman. *Systematic Theology.* 4 vols.

Vol. 1: *Introduction/Bible.* Minneapolis: Bethany House, 2002.
Vol. 2: *God/Creation.* Minneapolis: Bethany House, 2003.
Vol. 3: *Sin/Salvation.* Minneapolis: Bethany House, 2004.
Vol. 4: *Church/Last Things.* Minneapolis: Bethany House, 2005.

Geisler (1932–2019) was the dean of Southern Evangelical Seminary in Charlotte, North Carolina. This lengthy, detailed work is the culmination of his many years of teaching and writing, emphasizing a philosophical approach to theology but also giving attention to Scripture, the history of doctrine, and his critiques of modern liberal deviations from orthodox theology.

Griffith Thomas, W. H. *The Principles of Theology: An Introduction to the Thirty-Nine Articles.* 1930. 5th ed., rev. London: Church Book Room Press, 1956.

Although this book is structured around the Anglican (or Episcopalian) Thirty-Nine Articles, it functions well as a thoughtful introductory text in Christian doctrine even for those outside the Anglican tradition. It has been widely used in British evangelical circles for many years. Griffith Thomas (1861–1924) was principal of Wycliffe Hall, Oxford, and then professor of Old Testament at Wycliffe College, Toronto. He also played a role in founding Dallas Seminary just before his death.

Henry, Carl F. H. *God, Revelation, and Authority.* 6 vols. Waco, TX: Word, 1976–83.

This is a major work containing detailed interaction with hundreds of other scholarly positions. Henry (1913–2003) was a leading evangelical theologian with great strengths especially in the areas of apologetics and philosophical theology.

Hodge, Charles. *Systematic Theology.* 3 vols. 1871–73. Reprint, Grand Rapids: Eerdmans, 1970.

This major Reformed systematic theology is still widely used today. Hodge (1797–1878) was professor of systematic theology at Princeton Theological Seminary.

Horton, Michael. *The Christian Faith: A Systematic Theology for Pilgrims on the Way.* Grand Rapids: Zondervan, 2011.

Horton is a prolific author and a professor of systematic theology and apologetics at Westminster Seminary California. This is a clear statement of contemporary Reformed theology.

Horton, Stanley M., ed. *Systematic Theology.* Rev. ed. Springfield, MO: Gospel Publishing House, 1995.

Horton (1916–2014) was Distinguished Professor Emeritus of Bible and Theology at the Assemblies of God Theological Seminary in Springfield, Missouri. This book is a clear, carefully argued collection of eighteen chapters on topics in systematic theology by Pentecostal scholars.

Lewis, Gordon R., and Bruce Demarest. *Integrative Theology.* 3 vols. Grand Rapids: Zondervan, 1987, 1990, 1994. One-vol. ed., 1996.

Lewis and Demarest are both professors of systematic theology at Denver Seminary in Colorado, a Conservative Baptist seminary (Lewis retired in 1993). This is an excellent contemporary work that integrates historical, biblical, apologetic, and practical material with systematic theology.

Litton, Edward Arthur. *Introduction to Dogmatic Theology.* Edited by Philip E. Hughes. London: James Clarke, 1960. First edition published 1882–92.

This is a standard Anglican (Episcopalian) systematic theology by an evangelical British theologian of the nineteenth century. Litton lived from 1813 to 1897.

MacArthur, John, and Richard Mayhue. *Biblical Doctrine: A Systematic Summary of Bible Truth.* Wheaton, IL: Crossway, 2017.

MacArthur is the president and Mayhue the former vice president of the Master's Seminary in Sun Valley, California, where MacArthur also carries on a worldwide ministry of Bible exposition as the pastor-teacher of Grace Community

Church. This volume is clearly written and biblically based, with frequent application to life. MacArthur and Mayhue defend biblical inerrancy, believer's baptism, a Reformed view of salvation, and a cessationist view regarding spiritual gifts.

McGrath, Alister E. *Christian Theology: An Introduction.* 2nd ed. Oxford: Blackwell, 1997.

McGrath is a professor of science and religion at Oxford University and was previously principal of Wycliffe Hall, Oxford, research lecturer in theology at Oxford University, and research professor of theology at Regent College, Vancouver. The first part of this useful book (pp. 3–137) provides a clear overview of the history of doctrine. The second part (pp. 141–235) discusses sources and methods in theology. The last part (pp. 239–563) treats in topical order the subjects ordinarily covered in systematic theology, primarily with a wide-ranging survey of ancient and modern viewpoints on each subject. McGrath does not advocate a particular theological tradition in this book and instead explains that it "does not seek to tell its readers what to believe, but rather aims to explain to them what has been believed, and to equip them to make up their minds for themselves, by describing the options available to them and their historical origins" (xvi).

Miley, John. *Systematic Theology.* 2 vols. Library of Biblical and Theological Literature, vols. 5–6. New York: Eaton and Mains, 1892–94. Reprint, Peabody, MA: Hendrickson, 1989.

This is probably the most scholarly and extensive Arminian systematic theology ever written. Miley (1813–95) was a professor at Drew Theological Seminary in Madison, New Jersey.

Milne, Bruce. *Know the Truth*. Rev. ed. Leicester, UK;
    Downers Grove, IL: InterVarsity Press, 1998.

This thoughtful, clearly written evangelical guide to Christian doctrine has found wide use among students. Milne lectured in biblical and historical theology at Spurgeon's College, London, and then from 1984 to 2001 was senior minister of First Baptist Church in Vancouver, British Columbia, Canada.

Mueller, John Theodore. *Christian Dogmatics*. St. Louis,
    MO: Concordia, 1934.

This is a condensation and translation of Francis Pieper's *Christliche Dogmatik* (Christian Dogmatics) by a professor of systematic theology at Concordia Seminary in St. Louis, Missouri, a Missouri Synod Lutheran institution. It is an excellent statement of conservative Lutheran theology.

Murray, John. *Collected Writings of John Murray*. 4 vols.
    Carlisle, PA: Banner of Truth, 1976–82.
    _____. *The Imputation of Adam's Sin*. 1959. Reprint, Nutley,
    NJ: Presbyterian and Reformed, 1977.
    _____. *Redemption Accomplished and Applied*. Grand Rapids:
    Eerdmans, 1955.

Murray (1898–1975) was professor of systematic theology at Westminster Seminary in Philadelphia and one of the most articulate modern defenders of Reformed theology.

Oden, Thomas. *Systematic Theology.* 3 vols.

Vol. 1: *The Living God.* San Francisco: Harper & Row, 1987.
Vol. 2: *The Word of Life.* San Francisco: Harper & Row, 1989.
Vol. 3: *Life in the Spirit.* San Francisco: Harper & Row, 1992.

Oden (1931–2016) was a Methodist theologian who moved from his previous liberal theological convictions to a conservative evangelical position. He was professor of theology and ethics at Drew University in Madison, New Jersey. His method was "to make no new contribution to theology" but to ascertain and document the "consensual teaching" on which all the major figures and movements in the history of the church have agreed. This is a monumental work of great value, with thousands of quotations (especially from early Christian writers) on every aspect of systematic theology.

Olson, Arnold T. *This We Believe: The Background and Exposition of the Doctrinal Statement of The Evangelical Free Church of America.* Minneapolis: Free Church Publications, 1961.

This guide to Christian doctrine is based on the widely used statement of faith of the Evangelical Free Church of America. Olson (1910–2003) was the first president of the Evangelical Free Church.

Ott, Ludwig. *Fundamentals of Catholic Dogma.* Edited by James Canon Bastible. Translated by Patrick Lynch. St. Louis, MO: Herder, 1955. First published in German, 1952.

This was a standard textbook of traditional Roman Catholic theology.

Packer, J. I. *Concise Theology*. Wheaton, IL: Crossway, 2020; Leicester, UK: Inter-Varsity Press 2011.

This readable volume lives up to its name because Packer, an Anglican with strong Reformed convictions, is a master of saying much in a few words. From 1996–2016 he taught at Regent College in Vancouver, British Columbia, Canada. He died in 2020. He was one of the most widely respected and influential evangelical theologians of our time.

Pieper, Francis. *Christian Dogmatics*. 3 vols. Translated by Theodore Engelder et al. St. Louis, MO: Concordia, 1950–57. First published in German, 1917–24.

This is the standard systematic theology of conservative Lutheranism. Pieper (1852–1931) was a Missouri Synod theologian and professor and president of Concordia Seminary in St. Louis.

Pope, William Burt. *A Compendium of Christian Theology*. 3 vols. 2nd ed. New York: Phillips and Hunt, n.d.

This work, first published in 1875–76, is one of the greatest systematic theologies written from a Wesleyan or Arminian perspective.

Reymond, Robert L. *A New Systematic Theology of the Christian Faith*. Nashville: Thomas Nelson, 1998.

Reymond (1932–2013) was a professor at Knox Theological Seminary in Fort Lauderdale, Florida, and previously had taught for more than twenty years at Covenant Seminary in St. Louis, Missouri. This is a detailed, up-to-date systematic theology from a Reformed perspective. Reymond introduces many of his chapters with a relevant quotation from the Westminster Confession of Faith and places himself squarely within that theological tradition.

Ryrie, Charles. *Basic Theology.* Wheaton, IL: Victor Books, 1986.

This is a very clearly presented introduction to systematic theology from a dispensationalist perspective, written by a former professor of systematic theology at Dallas Theological Seminary. (Ryrie lived 1925–2016.)

Shedd, William G. T. *Dogmatic Theology.* Edited by Alan W. Gomes. 3rd ed. Phillipsburg, NJ: Presbyterian and Reformed, 2003. Originally published by Charles Scribner's Sons, 1889.

Shedd (1820–94) stood clearly in the Reformed tradition and taught at Union Theological Seminary in New York. This work has been widely used and highly valued, though it was previously available only in a difficult-to-use three-volume edition. Now it has been thoroughly edited and reorganized by Alan Gomes with the addition of clear section headings, an extensive glossary, and translation of all foreign language quotations. Gomes is chairman of the department of theology at Talbot School of Theology, Biola University, in La Mirada, California.

Strong, Augustus H. *Systematic Theology*. Valley Forge, PA:
    Judson Press, 1907.

Strong (1836–1921) was president and professor of theology
at Rochester Theological Seminary and, from 1905 to 1910,
was the first president of the Northern Baptist Convention.
This text was widely used in Baptist circles for most of the
twentieth century until being largely replaced by Millard
Erickson's *Christian Theology* (1983–85).

Swindoll, Charles R., and Roy B. Zuck, gen. eds. *Understanding
    Christian Theology*. Nashville: Thomas Nelson, 2003.

Ten different dispensational theologians (Robert Saucy,
J. Carl Laney, John Witmer, Robert Gromacki, Robert
Lightner, Robert Pyne, Earl Radmacher, Henry Holloman,
Edward Hayes, and John Walvoord) have written the ten major
sections of this book, which makes it an excellent recent statement of theology from a dispensational perspective. All ten
authors have ties to Dallas Seminary.

Thiessen, Henry Clarence. *Introductory Lectures in
    Systematic Theology*. Revised by Vernon D. Doerksen.
    Grand Rapids: Eerdmans, 1977. First published 1949.

This is an evangelical systematic theology textbook by
a former chairman of the faculty of the graduate school at
Wheaton College. Thiessen is Baptistic and dispensational in
theological perspective.

Wiley, H. Orton. *Christian Theology*. 3 vols. Kansas City,
    MO: Nazarene Publishing House, 1940–43.

This Arminian systematic theology by a respected theologian in the Church of the Nazarene is probably the best Arminian systematic theology published in the twentieth century, but it does not match John Miley's work in scholarly depth.

Williams, J. Rodman. *Renewal Theology: Systematic Theology from a Charismatic Perspective*. 3 vols. Grand Rapids: Zondervan, 1988–92. One-vol. ed., 1996.

Williams (1918–2008) was a charismatic scholar who taught at Regent University (formerly CBN University) in Virginia Beach, Virginia. This clearly written theology interacts extensively with the biblical text and other literature. It is the first systematic theology published from an explicitly charismatic perspective.

SCRIPTURE INDEX

SUBJECT INDEX